Making and Managing
High-Quality Workplaces
AN ORGANIZATIONAL ECOLOGY

Making and Managing High-Quality Workplaces

AN ORGANIZATIONAL ECOLOGY

Fritz Steele

Teachers College, Columbia University
New York and London

Published by Teachers College Press, 1234 Amsterdam Avenue,
New York, N.Y. 10027

Library of Congress Cataloging in Publication Data

Steele, Fritz.

　Making and managing high-quality workplaces.

　Includes index.
　1.　Office layout.　2.　Office practice.　3.　Work
design.　I.　Title.
HF5547.2.S74　1986　　　658.2　　　85-17386

ISBN 0-8077-2812-8 (paperback)
ISBN 0-8077-2777-6 (cloth)

Manufactured in the United States of America

91　90　89　88　87　86　　　1　2　3　4　5　6

To
Debbie, Lauren, and Graham

Contents

PART IV: FUTURE APPLICATIONS IN WORKPLACE MANAGEMENT

Introduction

We are clearly in a period where the old American "frontier" assumptions about abundance of resources and endless supplies of energy and materials are no longer valid (if they ever were). Every day groups of U.S. businesses are facing the hard fact that productivity has leveled off or declined and that growth will not be the cure-all — in other words, businesses must do better with the resources they already have, including people, materials, capital, and settings.

The nature of my consulting work is essentially a response to this challenge. I am attempting to help organizational leaders to do better with what they have, to improve the health and adaptability of both members and the system as a whole, so that there is a resilience that helps them to deal effectively with both good times and bad without degrading themselves or the organization in the process. To this end, an increasing percentage of my time has been spent in an area that has received relatively little conscious attention from middle and upper management teams. For reasons that I hope will become clear, I have chosen to call this area "organizational ecology," by which I mean the pattern of reciprocal relationships and influences among organizational members and their workplaces. I am really borrowing a term from the more developed field of animal ecology, where there is a strong tradition of research in the study of the relationships between animals and their settings. My intention has been to develop a similar understanding of the relationship between organizations and the settings in which they operate, so that better choices can be made about how to structure, use, and change these settings to satisfy both organizational and individual needs.

What I have been trying to promote with my clients is not a commitment to research projects per se but an awareness of the impact of organizational ecology, with the hope that this awareness will influence ways of thinking about problems and solutions related to productive design and use of workplaces. Included in this ecological point of view are four key areas of focus:

1. Variations in workplace layout and design and their effects on the individuals, groups, and organizations who use them
2. Organizational processes for creating, managing, and altering settings and how different organizations characteristically approach these processes
3. Patterns of use of workplaces; that is, the ways in which features of the physical setting and the social organization (policies, norms, values, and so on) interact to produce effective or ineffective modes of use
4. The nature of "work" as defined for managers and executives, and the ways in which this definition can be constrained or expanded by the nature of the workplaces in which they operate (and the ways in which the design of these workplaces is channeled by such definitions of managers' work tasks)

As I see it, organizational ecology is the area of reciprocal relationships between human organizations and their workplaces. It includes the impact of settings on individuals, groups, and the whole organization, and the influence of organizational "character" and dynamics on the design, management, and use of workplaces. Although I think that these influences are interesting in their own right, this book and my consultation efforts have a further purpose: to promote effective processes of workplace design and management that lead to high-quality work environments. By "high quality" I mean work environments that enhance the users' abilities and sense of self-worth, promote effective task accomplishment, "energize" users, reflect a spirit of place and identity, and can be adapted when users' needs change.

Perhaps more should be said about why I am concerned enough about this area to write a book about organizational ecology. I have worked for more than fifteen years as an organizational consultant, usually trying to help clients develop better means for spotting, diagnosing, and solving human organization problems. Because of my natural interest in architecture and design, I became more and more aware of the part played by the physical setting in influencing the dynamics of organizational life. I started to make recommendations about the physical shape as well as the social shape of my client organizations, since in practice they are part of the same ecological system. Managers may think of problems compartmentally as a "business" problem, a "personnel" problem, or a "facilities" problem, but in practice we all experience our world as a whole, so that the impact of any element would be different if the other elements were not also present in whatever form they take.

Having started with an emphasis on the impact of work settings on users, my consultations have gradually led me to expand my focus to the reciprocal process: how settings are designed and altered by users, and how they are used once they are occupied. This shift provides a more balanced view of the reciprocal relationship between people and their workplaces, so that effecting change becomes a question of how to break into the cyclical flow of people shaping settings that then shape them.

The two main goals of this book are (1) to add to the readers' understanding of how physical settings affect organizations and how organizational processes influence the shape of work settings, and (2) to provide some practical processes for making, altering, and managing high-quality work settings. Since I am also trying to expand the range of responsibilities that managers feel for work settings, the intended audience for this book is fairly broad: executives, managers, and other organizational members who potentially shape settings. In addition, this book will be useful for space planners, architects, and other designers whose effectiveness could be enhanced by a better understanding of organizational ecology and the dynamics of their client systems.

Reflecting my consulting experience, the majority of the examples and patterns discussed in this book relate most directly to office-type work: information processing, holding meetings, making decisions, generating reports, and sharing information either face-to-face or over the telephone. It is in offices that managers have tended to lag behind in paying specific attention to the need for systematic analysis and innovation when creating new work settings. Hospitals, factories, schools, and the like have all benefitted more from design innovations than has the basic office installation, even though office setups are by far the largest category of work settings in this country.

Many of the points of view expressed in this book can be applied to factories, laboratories, and other work settings, but usually with some very specific task and technological considerations appropriate to that setting. My purpose was not to explore each of these (nor was there space to do it), hence my general focus is on office-type installations.

VALUES AND ASSUMPTIONS

Since this book is a statement of my personal approach to understanding and using an organizational ecology viewpoint, I think it is important to articulate some of the primary values and assumptions on which this approach is based. These are fundamental points of view that have evolved through my experiences in observing and helping to change human organizations and their settings.

Values

Individual human beings have inherent worth and should be treated as such; they also have basic needs that must be met in order to survive and be healthy. An organization also has "needs" — certain functions and inputs that should be met in order for it to survive and fulfill a mission in its environment. Both individual and human systems needs should be considered in workplace design. There is not just one "right" answer as to which should be satisfied.

Management processes should enhance the sense of self-worth of members, not degrade it. People should be able to influence or control some elements of their immediate work surroundings, so they do not feel powerless and so they can get information back about the effectiveness of their choices over time.

Dealing with disagreements and conflicts in the open and developing skills to do this well are healthier alternatives than avoiding them, smoothing them over, or jockeying through hidden agendas with respect to spatial decisions. Learning from experience should be an explicit goal for most organizational processes; structures should be set up that promote this learning, not block it.

Assumptions

The following assumptions grow out of the above values:

1. An organization's leaders should be concerned about the match between the organization and its physical settings, and they should manage these settings on a more or less continuous basis, not just when there is an unavoidable crisis or mismatch.
2. Although it can cost time, money, and aggravation, it is still beneficial to provide opportunities for members of the work organization to exert personal control over their work settings.
3. A setting should be a positive contributor to the tasks being done in it, not a block to them.
4. A setting should be changed as the needs of the users and their modes of working change, rather than be left to become a detriment to their activities.
5. The organizational rules, policies, and norms about using a setting should enhance, not block, the efficient use of that setting by members.
6. First and foremost, a setting should be designed for its residents/users, not for display to occasional visitors, no matter how important these visitors may be.

7. Managers should try to create a work environment that is stimulating and alive rather than dull and "deenergizing" to its users.

8. A space management process should have feedback loops concerning the effects of both the setting and the space design process itself (such as a cycle of action→sensing→diagnosis and planning→experimentation→evaluation→action, and so on).

These values and assumptions seem to be fundamental to an ecological approach to workplace design and management. Without them (or some similar set of basic assumptions), it is hard to know how to assess the effects of workplaces and the processes being used to manage them.

THE FLOW OF THIS BOOK

There are several different sets of materials that have been combined in this book to describe the organizational ecology point of view and how to use it to create better workplaces. Part I is concerned with patterns in managing organizational settings and the social influences on workplace design and use. These include the impact of an organization's dynamics on the design and use of workplace resources; the effect of policies, procedures, and informal norms on the use patterns for work settings; the problems of choice of location for an organization; and control issues in the use and alteration of workplaces.

Part II describes specific processes for diagnosing, altering, and creating workplaces. These processes are based mainly on my experiences with clients in the last ten years. Although they are not the only viable models of how to do space planning and evaluation, they should be of practical value to executives and managers who want to become more aware of and to improve the processes of workplace design and management in their organizations.

Part III is concerned with the organizational impact of the way work settings are designed. This is the content that will be shaped through the methods presented in Part II. It describes some of the main effects of work settings and how these can be observed in order to assess the advantages and disadvantages of various layouts and designs. The main areas of impact that will be discussed are a sense of identity and ownership, social interactions, energy levels and excitement, task effectiveness and efficiency, power and influence, boundary relations, and organization climate and quality of work life experiences.

Part IV will look ahead and suggest some applications of the organizational ecology point of view to the future design of work settings. Here

I have selected topics that show how an ecological viewpoint can be useful in both recurring design problems that are with us today and in new situations that we can predict will become more prevalent in the near future. These topics include applications of organizational ecology to the design of settings for executive teams as well as for temporary task forces or teams, and for training and development activities. Future developments that are likely to occur in workplace design are new diagnostic techniques, new office technologies, and emerging changes in values and norms about work settings and their impact on users.

I hope you will dig into this book with an openness to new ways of looking at your settings, how you manage them, and what goals you try to satisfy through them. Even if this is not all that new to you personally, it can confirm that your views about work settings and their use do have a base in fundamental relationships between people and settings, although they may conflict with the ways workplaces have traditionally been managed in your own organization.

Part I

MANAGING ORGANIZATIONAL ECOLOGY

This first part is intended to set the stage for understanding organizational processes related to facilities design and management. Chapter 1 describes an ecological point of view for dealing with physical settings in organizations, while Chapter 2 recounts some of the most prevalent patterns and problems in the management of workplaces. In Chapter 3 I examine the ways in which the social dynamics of organizations influence the workplace design process, and Chapter 4 focuses on the impact of the social system (formal and informal) on the way workplaces are used by members and visitors.

CHAPTER 1

What Is
Organizational Ecology?

The mix of physical features in many American organizations is the result of a relatively unplanned set of separate decisions that tend to be made on the basis of habit, old assumptions, and hidden agendas held by those who influenced the decisions. Taken by themselves, each feature may have made some sense and served some purpose, but when one looks at the total pattern the effects of the setting are often to slow down work and to provide a working environment that feels out of step for many of the people who have to use it day after day. By contrast, the viewpoint of organizational ecology as it will be developed here suggests that effective workplace design and management include testing old assumptions and design solutions, as well as considering both individual elements and whole patterns of mutual influence among physical features, users, and organizational structures.

In seeking a way to provide an effective introduction to the viewpoint of organizational ecology, I decided to present a case example from my consulting experiences.

CASE EXAMPLE: MINZO, INC.

Several years ago I was asked to do an assessment of the working environment of an office building in New England. The building and its members were part of a high-technology firm I shall call Minzo, Inc. The company had a history of complaints about the building as a place to work. It was a low-rise building with two large floors of about 150,000 square feet each and a very small percentage of window area to wall surface.

The report I prepared for Minzo contained many of the issues and themes that will be discussed throughout this book. As I did my assessment, I looked not only at the physical features of the building but also

3

at the processes used to make design decisions and the patterns of use in the building. All these factors contribute to the overall sense of place that workers experience there.

The following is a summary of my initial report to the Minzo facilities manager. The building being evaluated is referred to here as "Minzo Park."

Diagnosis

Some Given Constraints.   There are a few features of the Minzo Park environment that may be considered to be given constraints, unless major expenditures are anticipated.

The building's occupants, groupings, and uses tend to change very rapidly, so that the current system of utilizing a mainly open-plan layout with screens makes more sense than building permanent, full-height walls that then shape what can be done and where.

Automobile access is severely limited at peak times, as is parking; this situation generates major employee frustrations at the beginning and end of each workday.

Because of the original, general-purpose nature of the Minzo Park building (which was created before the company knew how it was going to be used or by whom), the major climate control systems are based on covering large open spaces; tinkering with layout or the system itself tends to throw it out of balance. This accounts for the high frequency of complaints from users about the unpredictable temperatures.

The relatively small windows and their shape (vertical slits, essentially) will never provide very much natural light into the interior areas of the building.

Design.   The building lacks a center (or centers for subareas). There are few common spaces where people can interact informally without being on top of someone else's workplace or blocking a corridor.

Density varies widely around the building but is clearly too high in many areas, such as accounting (a function that typically is overcrowded), while too low in others.

Publicly shared areas such as passageways tend to be totally devoid of any decoration or signs of human influence; they are no-person's lands with little conscious design, like leftover space that is not supposed to count in users' experiences.

Many of the surfaces of walls and furniture are slick and hard, which increases reflections of both noise and glare from fluorescent lights.

There is a lack of sense of identity to the building as a whole and to most of the subareas. It is hard to get one's bearings in the building or to describe to someone how to find a particular group. This increases users' experiences of monotony and awareness of the building's large size.

There is an overall lack of design to layouts of work stations, especially in the way adjacent areas interface. The design of boundaries is almost random.

The entrance lobby appears hidden away (confusing to visitors) and very shabby in terms of furniture and graphics (which generates complaints from both visitors and members); this is definitely not a high-quality introduction to Minzo, Inc., nor a good way to start the workday.

Large areas of open-plan layout tend to have all screens of the same height, producing a dull, monotonous view across the sea of partition-tops. In those areas where screen heights vary, it appears to be totally related to status, with little regard for effective design principles for creating enclosure and privacy.

Decision Making About Design. Personal influence seems high over peoples' own desk and work area; members generally feel good about this nonuniformity, which fits the Minzo cultural traditions.

There is a lack of coordination in decisions that affect more than one area, however, such as public walkways or boundary walls. The alternatives do not get discussed, and members felt that the lack of a process for doing this reduced their influence over the atmosphere of Minzo Park.

A "hoarding" pattern exists where the "owner" of some assigned space will claim it all even when it is excessive, as a hedge against unpredicted growth (Minzo is a rapidly growing enterprise). This creates both dead spaces and unequal distributions of density based more on savvy at hoarding than on task needs.

It was not clear how often task needs (e.g., what will be done there) were taken into account in the layout of an area versus just how many bodies could be accommodated in the square footage available.

A committee was set up to work on the coordination of space decisions building-wide, but it seems not to have any influence over real space decisions if senior executives choose to circumvent or ignore it.

A company-based norm at Minzo implies that physical settings are not important and therefore money should not be spent on good design. In fact, managers are not supposed to create nice-looking work areas, even if they cost *less* than a more poorly designed layout because it would draw too much attention to a concern with design. People at Minzo should only pay attention to the "real" things, like their jobs (but contrast this with the strong hoarding pattern, which is very visible to members at all levels). This antidesign norm makes it hard to raise space issues, to change patterns of use of spaces when those patterns are ineffective, and to talk about organizational issues related to them.

Use Patterns.   Because of crowding and the lack of closed private offices, people feel that they cannot control interruptions and intrusions. Part of this frustration is caused by the way layouts are done — with little attention given to lines of sight, the relationships of desks to trafficways, and such. Intrusions also occur because the system lacks a norm of concern and respect for others' privacy; it also lacks a signal system for people to let each other know when they do not want to be interrupted.

Status is a big determinant in who can do what with their spaces, even though the official myth is that status is not a big concern for Minzo managers.

Recommendations

The main theme suggested by my observations would be to aim for *more conscious environmental management*: striving to do better at relating the design and use of Minzo Park to organizational structures, tasks, problems, and actual users' preferences and styles.

I would work to reduce hoarding and free up dead spaces, so that densities throughout the building will be more fairly distributed.

By creating some visible social structures (regular meetings, committees, forums), managers could raise and discuss issues underlying key space decisions or dilemmas.

More care should be taken to plan layouts of areas in a professional manner, keeping in mind what tasks are being done; who will interact with whom; which parts should be more or less open; where the greatest sources of noise will be; how people can be arranged so that they are accessible but not staring at one another; and how boundaries will be created, delineated, and managed. Soft, sound-absorbing surfaces should be the general rule whenever something new is added.

Some new community spaces should be created in central locations (so they will be used) to help reinforce the identities of subareas. These should be emphasized rather than the identity of the whole building, which is too large and has too many disparate groups in it whose only connection is their address.

Because of the frequency of changes at Minzo Park, flexible materials should be used, keeping as few fixed walls and other installations as possible. A process should be developed for making changes affecting adjacent groups, so that renovations are not always being done haphazardly.

Since one large group is due to move out of the building shortly, I would use this as an opportunity to plan that space in an experimental manner that would serve as a demonstration project for how to upgrade other parts of the building over time. This approach would look at both physical and social system structures: design, decision processes, use patterns, and norms about who can do what and where.

Graphics and Decorations. Special attention should be paid to the corridors and other shared-use paths (such as the walkway beside Personnel), and the wall surfaces should be used as an opportunity for interesting displays, not just left blank. This is especially important at centering spots on walls at the ends of a corridor or where a corridor jogs. Contact paper might be used to allow people to draw on the walls. The paper could be changed periodically to start fresh.

Signs. More care should be taken with signs and other graphics to designate group areas and routes through the building; the signs should have some distinct variations and not look alike at a distance (as is the case now).

Plants. More plants should be used to soften areas, provide visual interest to large areas of screened work stations, and supply screening and symbolic separation. The plants should not be placed in out-of-the-way corners where their screening function is wasted.

What If You Do Nothing Differently?

If the future design and planning process for Minzo Park is essentially like the past process, there are several likely outcomes. This will be a signal to users of Minzo Park that the corporation cares little about where and how members have to spend their waking hours. Morale will therefore not improve very much, even if densities improve somewhat because of the impending exit of one group (and past practice would suggest that the company will cram an even bigger group into that space). People feel that they are expected to accept a poor setting without the compensating excitement of being on the "frontier" as Minzo people were in the early days in the dilapidated building where Minzo started. (The norm about "environment is trivial" presumably sprang from this early period, when there was little choice anyway.)

I suspect that the user groups at Minzo Park will require more space in total and have higher costs for changes (which will be needed more frequently due to inadequate planning) than if a more systemic approach to place management were utilized.

The impending major move will be a missed opportunity to test the principles that could be applied to a more integrated space management process. It will also be a missed opportunity to deal with some of the underlying organizational issues (such as how fast the company should be growing in membership and who can control this rate) that get acted out in space planning conflicts.

MANAGEMENT PATTERNS

I have gone into considerable detail on the Minzo Park example because the report contained many of the themes that will be considered in depth in the following chapters. These themes are based on the organizational ecology viewpoint that a human organization is an ecological system whose health is determined by its balance of a number of factors: users' preferences and needs, users' activity patterns, the required action patterns of the organization (including major technology), the physical features of the organization's settings, the environments in which these settings are located, and the management decision processes that control the stability and rate of change of the settings.

This viewpoint takes spatial issues in an organization to a higher level than who wins or loses or what a "perfect" design would look like. The answers for ecological balance depend on the balancing of these forces in the system as a whole, not on one feature or solution that is going to be "good" for all time. My experiences in working with the facilities management process in different kinds of organizations would indicate that this viewpoint is still fairly rare in American businesses today. Instead, many leader groups tend to take a much less conscious, more hit-or-miss approach to designing and managing their work settings.

There are a number of relatively clear patterns in approaches to space management. First, executives tend to be aware of the need for conscious workplace management only when there is an obvious "problem"—running out of space, being in the wrong location, or using hopelessly outdated facilities that block the current tasks of the system. I believe, however, that workplace management should be a continuous process, with regular attention given to data collection, diagnosis, action, and assessment as a cyclical process.

Second, one of the reasons that attention to organizational ecology is sporadic (at best) is that most managers take relatively little responsibility for workplace management (and they are allowed to ignore it by their own bosses). They address the issue only when there is a real crisis or delegate it to a facilities manager. Often managers are not allowed to exert much control in shaping their own work settings since this is done by higher levels in the organization.

Third, when new workplaces are created, they are often based on old images, assumptions, and myths of what the organization needs, not on a current and forward-looking view of what the organization is becoming. Organizational leaders skip over the steps of looking at their own culture and structure, thereby failing to set goals for what they want to become and to create a design program that will help achieve these goals.

Fourth, many workplaces are created without the participation of the real users, so not only do their ideas not get into the design process but the process feels bad to them, since it is symbolic of their lack of power to influence surroundings in which they spend a good portion of their work life. The net result is that the workplace feels cold, hostile, or phony to many residents no matter how "good" the design is in some absolute or architectural sense.

In addition to these design *process problems*, which will be expanded upon in the next chapter, there are a number of specific design *content problems* that seem to crop up regularly in our work culture.

Organizations' office layouts often lack high-quality common areas that are central and accessible to members of the system. There is no appropriate area where members can interact informally without being in somebody else's way or in the middle of activities that require the area be kept clear (such as around a copying machine). If there are common areas, they are usually afterthoughts, located in leftover spots that are not accessible.

There is usually a heavy emphasis on status differentiations that are both expensive and inflexible. Many task-related changes in layout cannot be made because of the importance of status symbols (e.g., putting a manager in a central spot for the group versus in the high-status corner office out of the flow of action).

Boundaries between groups are often built too tight or too loose; their design is seldom based on a diagnosis of optional boundary conditions.

As organizational leaders search for efficient layout patterns, there seems to be an almost universal controversy over closed, private office layouts versus open-plan, landscape, or bull-pen arrangements. This issue generates a great deal of emotion, stubbornness, and posturing, but the battle seldom gets down to the core issues of the impact on individuals and on the system as a whole. It is necessary to sort these out as clearly as possible, relating them very concretely to the people and groups in question, in order to assess the relative merits of open or closed plans and make an informed choice.

Workplace design is often treated as mainly a programming problem: how to get X number of workers more or less permanently housed in Y amount of space, for the least cost in construction and maintenance. (This is also known as the *bag approach* — how many bodies can we stuff into this bag?) Much less attention is paid to the ecological effects on individuals, groups, and the organization as a whole. It is possible to have a very good quantitative fit in terms of amount of space and cost, yet have a very bad qualitative fit in terms of impact on organizational image and dynamics. This results in high costs that are hidden until the pinch becomes so obvious that it can no longer be ignored.

We will go further into problems of workplace design process and content shortly. The point here is simply that there are consistent patterns in the American work culture that need to be examined and changed. The current approaches to workplace design and management are not particularly effective; in many cases they are not conscious approaches at all, but afterthoughts. Thus we could repeat that the main goal of this book is to increase awareness of these processes and to provide some practical approaches to doing them better.

CHAPTER 2

Patterns and Problems in Workplace Design and Management

As stated in the first chapter, my consulting experience has given me the chance to observe many organizations' approaches to workplace design and management. I have seen enough cases to suggest some general patterns in the way facilities tend to be created and managed today, especially concerning typical issues and problems that are generated by such management processes. As further introduction to my view of organizational workplace management, a number of the most prevalent patterns in workplace design, management, and alteration will be considered.

INTERMITTENT MANAGEMENT

To me, the most important pattern in terms of its overall effect on facilities management is what we might call intermittent or "jerky" management of the people-settings interface. Top managers tend to deal with facilities issues in a very discontinuous fashion, searching for alternatives and taking action when someone is feeling some obvious "pinch" that can no longer be ignored. Up to that point, workplace environment issues, when raised by others in the organization, are dismissed as trivial, peripheral, or irrelevant to the "real" business decisions. (For example, a recent compendium called *The Management Handbook* has sixty-seven chapters on practical management areas, with none on managing space and facilities.[1])

The net result is that there is no real pattern of integrated facilities

---

[1]See Paul Mali (Ed.), *Management Handbook* (New York: John Wiley & Sons, Ronald Press, 1982).

plans, actions, evaluations, and replanning. Each problem, when it becomes severe enough, tends to be treated by itself, rather than as part of a flow of related problems and decisions. There are two costs associated with this pattern: (1) the obvious cost of false starts and inappropriate solutions that do not lead anywhere and must be torn out and redone as the needs of the system change; and (2) the many types of hidden costs of people doing day-to-day tasks in a setting that is not well suited to their needs, so that they are always making allowances or compromises with what they would do in an optimal environment. As stated in the first chapter, one of the primary themes throughout this book will be to stress the advantages of treating the workplace-people interaction as a continuous management responsibility, just like many other aspects of organizational action (people allocations to tasks, budgets, meetings design, personnel policies and procedures, and so on).

TOP-DOWN DOMINATION

The lack of responsibility that many managers feel for the continuous monitoring and improvement of their own groups' workplaces may to some extent be caused by a particular social system phenomenon: the tendency of the highest-level executives in American organizations to dominate facilities decisions. There is usually a great power imbalance around facilities, with the top members of the system tending to hold onto the "right" to make decisions that are at a much finer level of detail than in almost any other area of organizational life. The result is that most levels of the organization learn to take their workplaces as they are, assuming that they will have little choice about major variables such as size, location, and style of a facility. They, therefore, come to feel that these are somebody else's problems. In order to promote greater feelings of workplace management responsibility at all levels of an organization, we have to convince the top level to let go of some decisions and to reward (rather than subtly punish) those who are willing to take greater initiative and responsibility toward creating high-quality work settings.

Besides failing to encourage management responsibility toward creating quality workplaces, this pattern also produces some poor or inappropriate settings, especially when these settings are far removed from the top executives' own needs and experiences. Since top-level executives have difficulty getting accurate data about life far down in the organization, they tend to generalize from themselves or from idealized pictures of life at the lower levels. They have so much power over rewards and punishments, especially in terms of career opportunities for others, that they tend to see reflected back to them the picture that they signal to their subordinates (unconsciously, in most cases) that they want to be given. Thus their solutions in the area of workplace design tend to reflect an incomplete diagnosis of the problems they should be trying to solve. If the solutions work, it is in spite of this process, not because of it.

UNCLEAR DECISION AREAS

Even when top executives *want* to encourage initiative and participation in the creation of new workplaces, the process often seems to bog down in unclear goals, uncertain authorities, and tentative actions at all levels that fail to move the project along in a timely manner. This lack of success in trying to encourage participation by all levels in facilities decisions is primarily the result of an unclear decision matrix. By this I mean that top-level executives have not clearly identified different classes of decisions that have to be made (location of the facility, overall theme and scale, budget figures, relationships between different parts, themes in internal design, layouts of individual work areas, and so on) and designated who the appropriate people are to make them. They have not identified and communicated throughout the organization which decisions they want to hold as their own final determination, which they want to delegate to management below them, and which they want to encourage being made by the ultimate users themselves. The net result of such ambiguity is that people tend to wait for decisions or confirmation from the top, even about space issues that they could and should be deciding for themselves. They feel that it is safer not to act at all than to overstep vague lines of authority and make commitments that they later find were overruled or lamented by the organization's top power people. Thus, even if these top executives *intend* to have facilities decisions made at whatever level in the organization is most appropriate, it will not happen with much consistency unless they also create a relatively clear structure for defining classes of decisions and who should make them. (Specific recommendations for this process will be discussed in Chapter 6.)

LACK OF SYNCHRONIZATION OF DECISIONS

Even with the right people working on different classes of decisions, there is an additional type of problem: making facilities decisions and commitments at the appropriate time, when there is good information that leads to a good decision, but not so late that the timing throws the schedule off and backs up future tasks significantly. Because of the need for timeliness and information, managers tend to either delay decisions too long in order to have maximum information and therefore feel more sure of the parameters they use, or to make decisions too early because of the fear of not meeting the schedule. Unfortunately, trying to "bank" time by deciding early does not necessarily speed up the overall schedule (since it will still be controlled by other limiting factors), and it often produces poor decisions that are made with more uncertainty than was necessary.

EMPHASIS ON CONSPICUOUS COSTS

Workplace management processes have always suffered from the tendency for facilities managers and other decision makers to overemphasize the conspicuous, most visible cost associated with construction or change of settings. The most easily quantifiable factors, such as initial cost per square foot or monthly maintenance costs, receive a great deal of attention. Less quantifiable factors, such as a setting's toll on morale over the years of use or the increased energy and time needed to compensate for a bad layout, get discounted or ignored altogether when comparisons or tradeoffs are being made in the planning process.

This is not surprising, since managers seem to be inclined to weight quantifiable factors much more heavily than qualitative ones in most decision processes. This is a tendency that needs to be resisted if an organization is going to have effective workplace management, however, since the variables to be considered range from easily specifiable to extremely vague, with some of the vague ones having a very strong impact on the overall spirit of place that is created.

I suspect that the overreliance on quantifiable factors is in part caused by a too narrow conception of the variety of functions that settings play for their users. This narrowness leads to stereotyped notions about good and bad workplaces and to a lack of awareness of the variety of effects on individuals, groups, and the organization as a whole. An additional factor is the typical reward system set up for project and facilities management. Facilities people perceive this system as penalizing schedule slippage or increased cost, but not rewarding positive impact on organizational climate, group interaction, or other behavioral variables.

SPATIAL DECISIONS AND
HIDDEN ORGANIZATION CONFLICTS

An insidious factor that confuses workplace decisions is the intrusion of other organizational conflicts that people are not willing to deal with openly. For example, in a system where managers are adding new employees at a rate that alarms top management, the top management may try to stem this inflow by creating or holding to facilities that just do not allow any space for new people. This may or may not be a good design, but it has been chosen, not for functional reasons, but simply as a mechanical means of winning a disagreement that cannot be resolved openly. There are numerous examples of this type of hidden agenda controlling workplace design, and the next chapter will deal in part with how to recognize certain spatial design conflicts as likely indicators of other organizational issues that are being acted out indirectly.

UNCLEAR GOALS AND PARAMETERS

It is hard to develop and maintain an effective workplace management process when an organization's leaders do not have a coherent, agreed-upon set of goals and parameters for where they are trying to lead the organization. Sometimes these are lacking in both quantitative and qualitative terms; sometimes they have been developed for quantitative measures (such as increased sales, growth in numbers of employees) but not for more qualitative areas (such as the sense of mission, organizational structure, organizational climate, management philosophy/style, and goals for developing the basic capabilities of the organization and its groups).

The point here is that if there are basic agreements about these areas, it is much easier to work out meaningful facilities creation and management plans that really tell people something they can use in their planning of facilities, policies, and maintenance programs. Without a context set by overall directions and values, detail decisions seem to end up either being arbitrary and unrelated to each other or favoring those who are most skillful at the resource-allocation game. Since there are no coherent shared principles, such decisions become more tests of political power within the system than attempts to relate the parts to the whole.

BUILDING MONUMENTS TO THE PAST

A visible outcome of the lack of goal clarity is the tendency to create new settings that are testimonials or monuments to what the organization used to be with very little connection to what its leaders are striving to have it become. The absence of forward-looking goals, and particularly of articulated goals for development and change, leads managers to base their projections, layouts, and designs on the current mode of operation, with little perceived reward for real innovation and relatively high perceived risk of trying something new that might come off mixed (some pluses and some minuses) in the eyes of higher management. Without a conception of what they are trying to become, an organization's leaders tend to generalize from what is known, thereby creating a setting where everyone may physically be able to fit as individuals, but where many of the newer kinds of management tasks, interactions, and so on have no place to happen. This is at the heart of the view of organizational ecology that I am presenting here: the setting influences organizational life and performance in many visible and many not-so-visible ways. The more a new workplace is simply an extrapolation from the old, the more it will tend to be a drag on organizational changes in philosophy, goals, and management style. It pays to work on developing a shared picture of what these should be as an input into the design process.

Another reason for the monuments-to-the-past pattern is the tendency to focus on conspicuous cost and gains. Managers tend to take what they have as the given or standard, so that the value of changes has to be "proved" to them quantitatively ("Show me that my bottom line will be improved") before they will make significant changes in design concepts for their areas. In fact, their current workplace design may have significant hidden costs as they grow and change — costs that do not really get factored into the equation very easily when they are trying to decide about changes. (Yet I have never heard anyone say, "Prove that our present configuration is effective.") My guess is that this conservative bias actually costs a dynamic organization more than would any reasonable amount of experimentation.

UNDERUTILIZING THE WORKPLACE
MANAGEMENT EXPERIENCE

One of the reasons that the workplace management process has not been developed or integrated with other key management areas is the tendency in most companies to compartmentalize it as simply having to do with the creation, purchase, and maintenance of things — a necessary but essentially menial task that is best done as simply as possible. As can no doubt be inferred from the discussion so far, I think this view is not only too simplistic but actually misleading. It implies that people's skills, judgments, and feelings are switched on or off depending on the obvious importance of the issues with which they happen to be dealing at the moment. I think that the opposite is in fact true: people experience their world as a flow of experiences, as a whole as well as parts, and any or all of these experiences can contribute to both a sense of self-worth and a sense of increasing skill and mastery.

This view leads directly to the notion that processes and problems related to workplace design and management should be thought of not just as problems but also as opportunities — opportunities to develop skills in goal setting, diagnosing problems, scanning for acceptable and innovative solutions, resolving conflicts, and managing projects in an efficient and timely manner. For all these skill areas, workplace management provides a relatively concrete medium where the effects of one's choices are much more visible and tangible (if more than simple dollar costs are considered) than in many other arenas of work life.

"DENSE" RULES AND POLICIES
ABOUT USE OF FACILITIES

Even if an organization's members develop a good process for designing their facilities, they may end up watering down the contributions such facilities can make to the performance of the system. They do this through the rules and policies they establish about the *use* of the facilities: when and how spaces can be used and by whom, what authority it takes to gain access to a resource, what individuals can or cannot do to influence their own immediate work settings, what groups can do to decorate or alter their total spaces, and so on. The total social environments that guide such uses (policies, rules, informal norms, and habits) tend to be not so much designed as evolved through a mix of planned controls and historical accidents. It is an open question whether an organization's members are using their setting effectively and, if so, whether they are doing it because of or in spite of the rules and procedures that have been set up by management. In my experience, many groups could improve their organizational ecological balance simply by examining the ways in which their norms and policies affect the use of existing settings. If it works, it is certainly a cheaper solution than getting into a long-term building program to renovate or create a whole new workplace. And, in many cases, the same old policies and norms automatically grafted onto the new workplace (plus additional constraints because the setting is new and is supposed to be kept looking that way) tend to neutralize the potential payoff in creating the new setting. As we will discuss later (in Chapter 4), redesigning the physical setting is only making *half* a change; if it is going to produce the results expected, some supportive social system changes will also have to be instituted.

UNRESPONSIVE SETTLING-IN PROCESSES

The last common workplace management process problem that will be singled out here is one that occurs in the period just after people have moved into a newly created environment. There are always problems with such a move and with the post-move settling-in process. Planners and builders need to make adjustments to features that could only be set up approximately until the actual users were in residence, and the users themselves need to become accustomed to the quirks and possibilities of their new surroundings. The problems of this post-move period are not really unusual; they are the natural result of such a change. The new occupants need to be helped to make the adjustments as a normal step in the process, not as something unusual that signals a crisis or failure in design.

Unfortunately, facilities managers and project leaders who were primary agents for creating the new setting can feel very defensive about it, especially if there were some controversial choices they had to make and sell to the eventual users. Those who created the setting, in their desire to see it work well, can perceive users' reactions, concerns, and requests for help as simply "a lot of griping and sniping by people who ought to just shut up and give the whole thing a fair chance for a time before they start nit-picking it" (a quote from one facilities manager). They therefore tend to be relatively unresponsive to requests for help or adjustments; this, in turn, tends to give the new users a bad feeling about the whole start-up process and sours their feelings about the project. In the end they *do* tend to become more rejecting of it and less likely to give it a fair chance.

The antidote to this cycle, as I see it, is for the project teams to consider the post-move tinkering period to be an extremely important part of the design and construction process. As will be described in Chapter 7, I believe that they should take particular care to create a responsive structure that encourages users to raise problems early as a natural part of settling into the new setting.

CONCLUSION

The eleven patterns described above constitute my proposed list of the most prevalent problems in the workplace design and management process in the typical American work organization. The impact of these problems obviously varies from organization to organization. I suspect that some organizations could be characterized by dominant styles in the ways they typically approach workplace management issues: in one, people are generally thought of as furniture to be arranged like sofas and end tables; in another, spatial decisions are seen as cutting up turf and get made solely on the basis of power politics and jockeying for position (figuratively and literally, in the sense of trying to get oneself located near the perceived seats of power); in another, there is a sort of "Earth Mother" approach that seeks to make every individual warm and cozy, even if, as a result, the social groupings do not work well. The next chapter will examine key organizational dynamics that shape the character of workplace management.

CHAPTER 3

How Organizational Dynamics Influence Workplace Design and Management

SETTINGS-MANAGEMENT STYLES

The structure and internal dynamics of an organization strongly affect the way that organization's settings are created and managed. This point is a familiar (and often touchy) one to any designer who has worked with corporate clients, since on such a project one is bound to sense that the decision processes and responses of client representatives seem to be driven as much by unseen forces and assumptions as they are by the design problem. These forces may include power relationships, historical myths and experiences, relations between groups, management values and style, dominant reward systems, and key norms and values, all of which can influence how settings are created and managed.

Organizations differ considerably as to how effective they are at identifying, acquiring, and using needed resources in the creation and management of physical workplaces. In my work, I have seen many different approaches to this process, including the following relatively frequent styles of corporate-settings management.

The Nobody's Problem/Everybody's Problem Model. This may be the most prevalent style, which could also be called the "Pinch Model." Nobody pays much attention to overall facilities issues for long periods of time. When a significant problem or pinch emerges, then many executives or managers become concerned, often competing to sell their own favorite solutions. Attention to the issue is considerable until there is a resolution, and then most managers go back to their "real work." Over time, this style produces an intermittent, on-off approach to facilities management, not a planned process that has a consciously chosen shape to it.

20

The Key-Influentials Model.   This pattern consists of a few top executives taking a regular and personal interest in the design of their organization's work settings. Their concern is fairly constant, and they exert a lot of influence on facilities decisions, in many cases retaining final approval for themselves in both large-scale and detail-oriented decisions. They want to assure that their system's workplaces have a consistent, integrated feel that reflects their goals, values, and style as top executives. They tend to become the final arbiters of both design taste and task needs. They usually believe that their own experiences and views are representative of everyone else's in the organization. Thus they feel in a position to decide many issues with others' best interests and needs in mind, but they have little desire to check whether their assessments of those interests are accurate.

The Custodial Model.   In this management process, facilities design and management are still ultimately controlled from the top of the hierarchy, but the hands-on, day-to-day control is vested in a facilities or maintenance unit that usually answers only to the top executives. Most line managers are not expected or allowed to influence their settings very much. The facilities service group usually tends to be less responsive to the task and human needs of facilities users and to be mainly oriented toward a "custodial" view of their function — keep the facilities from being hurt by users and keep costs to a minimum. This approach is fairly predictable, since these are the dimensions by which the success of the facilities function is measured. Top executives are more concerned about not losing control and not letting "chaotic" settings decisions occur than they are about whether their subordinate managers are able to shape work settings effectively. Usually some lip service is given to the latter goal, but performance reviews and reward systems emphasize the custodial approach. Interestingly, I have run into a number of facilities managers who are actually former military people, presumably interested in facilities management because they like the relatively concrete, hands-on nature of the position and the requirements of orderly methods in order to keep track of what is happening with an organization's physical facilities.

The Flux Model.   In this mode, facilities management is spread throughout the organization so that there is more encouragement (and opportunity) for managers to use facilities as a tool to help them achieve results. There is less control from the top, but there is also relatively little *direction setting* about physical environment from the top executive group. As a consequence, physical choices that are made are better suited to the needs of user groups, but there is usually not much of an overall framework or theme to provide a consistent context for such decisions. They therefore tend to reflect independent subgroups' needs and to be heavily influenced by external inputs such as current fads in facilities design. The "hot" items in design tend to get used but are discarded just as quickly since there is no long-term strategy to encourage managers to follow through for a sufficient period of time to really test a particular design or set of assumptions.

The Nested-Participation Model. I have come across a few organizations whose leaders have attempted to develop and operate an overall facilities design/management process that helps people at different levels to influence their own settings. Their approach is to do this in the context of (or be "nested" in) a longer-term strategy that defines several factors: facilities management goals, basic assumptions about the organization's appropriate physical shape and relationships with its environment, types of decisions that are possible and appropriate for different levels of the organization, and how the quality of fit between settings and user groups can be monitored on a regular basis. These goals are often achieved through volunteer task groups that cut across formal group boundaries, broad-based surveys that collect data at all levels about changing needs for facilities, management sessions that generate new ideas about solutions to facilities problems, and performance reviews for managers that include dimensions related to effective facilities management.

Implications

It should be obvious that I think that the Nested-Participation Model is the most promising of the five models described here. It reflects a concern for conscious planning and action, rather than letting a big piece of organizational life simply happen in a jerky, chance manner. It also takes into account that people at different levels of the hierarchy and in different functions have different information, needs, problems, and perceptions of their own and others' experiences. These differences require that facilities management be thought of as the management of a resource closely tied to other organizational social processes, rather than simply treated as a prerogative of a top executive's fiefdom or a necessary hassle that should be dismissed as quickly as possible. Part II will discuss specific lessons that have been learned about the nested participation process in practice and some of the key pitfalls to making it work.

One of the crucial factors that makes such a process work is the identification and inclusion of people who can serve it as resources. You need to know which members at different organizational levels have useful strengths and abilities, such as awareness of spatial issues, an interest in environment and behavior of interior design, experience with building processes, and a desire to influence the shape of individual and group workplaces. In addition, there needs to be a clear message from the top of the system that it is legitimate (not insubordinate or nosy) for people to care and want to contribute to the process of workplace design and management. The clearest statement of such legitimacy is the creation of a structure that makes it easy, not difficult, for people to contribute. It also helps to create conditions that promote experimentation, change, and the seeking of feedback from users about the effects of such efforts.

SPACE DESIGN CONFLICTS AND
UNDERLYING SYSTEMIC ISSUES

The dominant pattern in most of the above models is one of holding onto control and influence over facilities design and use. In some it is just the top layer of the organization that holds on, in others it is the next layer of management or a designated facilities function that feels that they "own" it all. My experiences have suggested that this holding on is often driven less by seeking positive goals than by avoiding the perceived negative consequences of opening up the spatial influence process to more levels of the system. What do executives fear would happen? A variety of possible disasters seem to lurk in their minds, such as *general chaos*, as everybody does their own thing in a disorganized, unrelated manner; *embarrassment for managers*, as their groups make more demands and expect more responses from the hierarchy; *big delays* in decision making and getting workplaces built and occupied; *conflicts* over expectations and preferences for design of groups' areas; and an *inability to resolve these conflicts* at reasonable costs in time and energy.

These fears are certainly possible outcomes of opening up the workplace design process to wider participation and influence; some executives have undoubtedly had bad experiences that turned them against that sort of process. However, I believe that most of these fears can be satisfactorily answered or neutralized, given proper design of the process and a strong effort to identify who should appropriately make inputs to which classes of decisions. The specifics of such a process will be described in Part II.

There is one aspect of these common fears that deserves immediate attention here. Spatial decisions are not so difficult in themselves, but they are hindered by other factors in the organizational culture due to a general lack of openness about disagreements and conflicts. The workplace setting, because of its concrete, visible nature, becomes a focus for acting out unresolved issues that have not been dealt with by the system's normal management processes. From my consulting experience, it is obvious to me that conflicts about space design are often very heated and likely to become stalled because of hard positions that have a strong emotional base. These conflicts are a surface reflection of underlying systemic issues that people do not recognize or do not wish to discuss openly. Obtaining a genuine commitment to facilities decisions often requires dealing with the underlying issues that have been blocking resolution. The following are the focuses of the most typical workplace design conflicts, together with the likely organizational issues that tend to lie behind them.

Basic Themes of Decoration.   When basic decoration — furniture items, colors, fabrics, and the like — becomes a polarized issue, this often reflects a split within the organization over the long-term direction of the system, especially in terms of pressing for changes versus maintaining stability and upholding traditions. The specific design conflicts often show up in terms of the "traditionalists" versus the "modernists," where each group is trying to communicate (and institutionalize) what they think is the right approach to handling pressures for change within the system (and from without). There can be fierce disagreements around subjects such as having traditional desks versus "work stations," having a lot of wood in offices, using bright colors and graphics versus subdued colors and representational pictures on the walls, using innovative lighting systems versus traditional fixtures, and anything else where one group can identify themselves as progressive or traditional in relation to the other. The direction that "wins," once translated into a physical place, can then be a continuing reminder of a way of thinking about the future of the organization (stable versus changing) and therefore becomes a force for that direction, even though not consciously chosen in any open decision process. It may also be a continual reminder to the "losers" that they have to live in the middle of the symbols of their defeat, and this can continue to irritate them for years.

Increasing or Decreasing Space.   The dispute between moving into more space versus keeping present allocations generally has its roots in different views of members about the desired rate of growth of the whole operation. Some feel that growth is good (and in fact feel that it is essential for generating the excitement they want), while others feel that growth is risky and should only happen in a very controlled, planned manner. In one firm the key department heads kept expanding their activities and hiring more people to keep up with a booming market, while the president felt that their growth could come back to haunt them when the boom tailed off. He kept trying to get them to limit voluntarily their hiring of new people. This had little effect, so he finally tried another tactic: refusing to approve the expense of a move to larger quarters — in effect, putting a curb on growth simply by making it clear that there would be severe overcrowding problems if his department heads continued to hire. This did not resolve the underlying issue, but it certainly put the pressure on the space allocation process, and on his subordinates as well.

I have also seen the reverse polarization of this issue, where business had diminished and the polarization is over whether to stay in current (too large) spaces or move to smaller quarters. The underlying system issue here has to do with disclosure (e.g., admitting that a company has shrunk and that it is not just a temporary setback but likely to be a real shift downward in the scale of operation) versus avoiding the fact of shrinkage. It is also concerned with energy management — those who advocate the move feel that staying in the old too-large quarters can be depressing and remind everyone of the past and its successes compared with the present. They fear that the vitality of the organization will be further sapped by the depression, creating a downward spiral.

Closed- versus Open-Plan Layout.   The dispute over having closed work spaces or an open-plan layout is probably the most widespread spatial issue in American white-collar organizations today. As costs of materials and space continue to escalate, organizations are forced to do more with less, which naturally leads to the possibility of designing groups of flexible work stations separated by screens rather than fixed offices for all key members. The original costs of such an open-plan layout may or may not be less than a conventional closed layout, but the expenses over the full life of a location are demonstrably lower in terms of changes, maintenance, reorganization, flexibility of use, regrouping, and so on.

When the battle for closed offices versus open-plan work stations is waged, it is usually discussed by the closed-office advocates as strictly a "privacy" issue — they demand to have a private space for themselves. Behind this spoken theme are two that do not get discussed as openly. One is the polarization between those who value high disclosure as a means of relating to one another, and those who believe that an organization must be operated mainly through carefully controlled disclosure and secrecy. The high disclosure–low disclosure split is a deep one, since it requires the taking of a high-disclosure stance even to discuss it in the first place. The stronger the split, the less likely this is to happen.

The second below-the-surface theme is a split in terms of those people with high needs for physical status symbols and those with low needs or who believe that office layouts should not be used as rewards. The question is whether spatial arrangements should inherently reflect one's position in the system or if facilities should be arranged mainly on the basis of task needs and impact on social system dynamics. The split could be described as that between the elitists and the egalitarians or functionalists. It is very hard for an executive group to resolve this dispute if they themselves are split, and a satisfactory resolution usually requires a strong stand from the leader of the system.

Location of an Organization. The question of where a firm should be located, or whether it should move from its present location, is always driven by a combination of forces pushing in different directions. The underlying system issues can be many and varied for this one. One typical tension, however, concerns the question of the identity or mission of the organization — who are we and what are we trying to do? A polarization often develops between those who want to maintain and preserve the traditional identity of the system — "what we were and always will be" — and those who see that identity changing and want to accent it by moving to a location that communicates "what we are becoming and should be." Concurrent with this split, there may be other polarizations that have to do with values, change or stabilization, growth or maintenance of size, and so on, relating to the previously mentioned conflicts.

Assignment of Offices and Territories. At one level, disputes over who gets which offices and territories do represent a simple matter of people struggling for what they want. However, what they want is not always just the physical spot — the site often represents something more fundamental. Arguments over office location, for example, are likely to have heavily symbolic overtones, especially concerning who will be close to the highest-power people or units. The struggle is over who can make a claim to being central to the system's activities, and a way to stake that claim is to be physically central.

At a higher level, disputes over departmental territories can be driven by boundary conflicts, where groups are trying to control and manage their own boundaries (define the limits of insiders and outsiders for themselves) versus having these definitions thrust upon them by someone else. Because of this hidden issue, group members can become very agitated about what seem to be relatively trivial decisions concerning doors, filing cabinet locations, accessways, where secretaries will sit, and so on. These all represent concrete opportunities to demonstrate to oneself that one can control one's own boundaries and therefore one's fate.

Another source of office-claim disputes is a confusion between person and positional attributes, so that people become very eager to have their offices increase their perceived importance in a visible, tangible manner. They also feel that individuation is not particularly valued, so that people will be responded to in terms of what their places are like, almost as if their places were them. The more this tends to be true in an organization, the more stake people will feel in fighting for a particular office, location, or type of work station.

Luxuriousness of Furnishings.   The degree of luxuriousness that should be achieved in furnishing a workplace is often discussed as a question of costs (extravagant versus economical) or of image (successful or lean and Spartan). These may indeed be the splits that drive this conflict. There is another that may also be working at a deeper level — the question of how much of a difference there should be in the furnishings of high-power and low-power people in the system. This comes into play because the luxury is usually unevenly distributed (to say the least), with the top members receiving the lion's share. The issues are how big these differences should be, how visible they should be, and what the process will be for justifying these differences to the lower-power members.

The above instances illustrate the potential complexity of organizational conflicts over spatial features and arrangements. They usually are a result of concrete decisions that must be made (e.g., where to be located as a firm) *plus* some underlying system issues that are being acted out through this medium. A person who is trying to help the design process along should keep both of these in mind and be ready to work at both levels; each of them is real and important.

SPATIAL CHANGES AS DIAGNOSTIC INTERVENTIONS

Because spatial conflicts are often indicators of system dynamics, specific changes in facilities can serve as a medium for sharpening issues and learning more about an organization's characteristic problems and stresses. Settings are a good vehicle for this because they are so visible and concrete and because they tend to spark relatively strong preferences in people. It is therefore easy to monitor the reactions to a particular move.

Some of these diagnostic moves are relatively short term and can be done without great expense or fanfare. Relocating a new team to temporary quarters where the members are all together can very quickly generate data about how similar or different they are from one another.

This information would emerge over a much longer period of time if they remained scattered in their previous offices. Putting up or reducing barriers to movement is another move that tends to generate quick reactions. People will complain about or reinforce this act depending on their own preferences and images of the system. This provides a graphic picture of who feels connected with whom and where members think the boundaries should be drawn between different parts of the system.

Changing the nature of personal offices (or proposing that they be changed to a less private, more flexible work station concept) will generate extremely quick responses and give a feel for how connected members feel they are (and want to be) to one another, as well as whom they picture as "insiders" and "outsiders." Similarly, proposing a new policy about who can and cannot use particular facilities will provide a test of who defines that setting as their own, and whether there is much meaningful differentiation among groups or levels in the system. Conversely, declaring the end to exclusive use of an area by one group will generate reactions that suggest how well or tenuously the previous "owners" feel they are tied to the rest of the system. Even such simple actions as putting up a poster or picture can sometimes provoke surprisingly strong countermoves from facilities managers or higher executives, smoking out a previously hidden assumption about who deserves to be able to control their own workplaces.

Some physical interventions are more significant because they are more costly and take longer to implement. Proposing or effecting the move of an organization to a new and different type of location is sure to spark significant controversies that can be used as data about other conflicts within the system (as discussed earlier). Creating new traffic patterns in a building will change boundary management conditions for a number of groups, and watching what they do in response can tell much about where the psychological boundaries exist in members' minds. Sociotechnical changes in work processes and the social groupings to accomplish them will generate new data about people's style preferences, their attachments to one another, their assumptions about how such decisions should be made (and by whom), and their general stance toward change or stability as the best approach to life in the firm.

Changes in layout philosophy can make groups of people more (or less) visible than they have been to others in the past, which sometimes exposes a state of lethargy or depression that had gone unnoticed before. A similar result can come from grouping people together who had been scattered around a building: if there had been a common pattern of structured time wasting and unfocused activity, it can become visible because people see each other regularly, whereas before each individual did not know that other members were doing it too.

Of course, using longer-term, more elaborate physical changes as diagnostic events would not be done simply to see what would happen but rather for specific reasons that are deemed to be important at the time. What I am suggesting is simply that double mileage can be obtained: the effects and reactions can be used as diagnostic information about the state of the system and important systemic issues, rather than dismissed as merely the carpings of people who are resisting changes that are really in their own best interests. Unfortunately, the typical stances of executives and facilities planners who are fixed on seeing that things get done quickly is usually skewed in the direction of dismissal rather than diagnosis and learning about the system.

SUMMARY

To sum up briefly, organizations' dynamics influence the ways facilities are designed and managed. Styles of handling facilities management include five models: Nobody's Problem/Everybody's Problem, Key Influentials, Custodial, Flux, and Nested Participation. Recurring space conflicts tend to reflect underlying, undiscussed system issues. Such conflicts include how to decorate, whether to acquire more space, working in closed offices versus open-plan layouts, where the organization should be located, who should get which spaces, and how luxurious the work setting should be. In addition, more data about organizational issues can be gathered by observing what happens when physical changes are made, such as putting a scattered group together or tightening boundaries between different parts of the organization. The reactions can be opportunities to learn if they are not dismissed as irrelevant problems to be suppressed.

CHAPTER 4

Social Influences
on the
Use of Workplaces

When we think of a work organization as an ecological system where members interact with each other and with their physical environment, it is clear that creating effective workplaces is not solely a matter of building physical structures. A significant portion of people's experiences in their workplaces is shaped by the social context in which a setting is actually used by its residents. Therefore, if you want to promote changes in an organization to improve members' experienced quality of work life or sense of place, you should start with a diagnosis of the social system factors (policies, rules, social norms, and such) that are influencing or limiting the effective use of the setting. As a change target this area is usually cheaper (in capital outlay terms) and less messy (physically) than doing major physical alterations. With this potential in mind, we will explore some of the primary social factors that control the ways members use organizational settings.

FORMAL ORGANIZATIONAL POLICIES

The written rules that organizational leaders have established constitute that organization's formal policies concerning appropriate and inappropriate uses of the system's facilities. Some policies prescribe restrictions on certain types of facilities: who can reserve conference rooms, use the corporate training facility for conferences, hold large gatherings in the company dining room, park in the parking lot nearest the main entrance, use the computer room or remote terminal locations, eat in the various dining rooms (if there are several), or use the corporate exercise facility.

Another type of policy details the personal workplace elements available to people at different levels of the hierarchy — the status symbols. These symbols are usually elaborate, well defined, and likely to be strongly defended. Deviance from the policy (such as someone painting his door red when he is not yet entitled to a red door) usually evokes swift action to stamp out the anomaly. The maintenance department (which has been too overburdened to do routine maintenance) immediately manages to supply someone to show up unrequested and paint the red door white again. Policies about access to scarce facilities (e.g., the exercise room, the executive dining room, executive washrooms) also relate to the use of status symbols.

Having to maintain a consistent pattern with respect to who deserves which facilities and trappings can be a great block to effective and adaptive use of work settings. Requiring an executive to install a large battleship of a desk in his or her office because the position "deserves it" (read that *requires* it) can totally thwart spontaneous small meetings that the owner would like to be able to hold in that office. Another costly constraint is the pattern of rules (formal and informal) about high-status locations and therefore where high-ranking group members (such as the boss) must be located. Putting the boss in a corner office with two windows immediately rules out many other ways of arranging the physical relationship between boss and group members, such as having the boss in a central spot with the group around it. These same rules make it difficult to rearrange people's locations for temporary team groupings, since several people would have to occupy spots that were of higher or lower status than they were entitled to. As long as the rules are rigidly followed, spaces become unusable and people tend to be kept in their old locations even though it constrains the kinds of team interactions they should be having in order to do their jobs well. A similar result comes from having private offices for people who travel a great deal away from their main location: unless there is a rule or norm about temporary access to such vacant spots, the system has to maintain a significantly larger physical plant than necessary for the average number of people in the building at any given moment.

Another important set of policies is concerned with the latitude allowed to individuals and groups in influencing or altering their immediate work environments. Some organizations' leaders spell this out in some detail, explicitly saying what *is* allowed (personal pictures, mementos) and what is *not* allowed (bringing in furniture or rugs from home, hanging up posters, repainting the walls of an office or group's area without approval, and so on). In other organizations only the don'ts are spelled out, and the implication is that most other decorative acts are all right *if* they are in keeping with the character of the company (which can sometimes be a big "if").

These types of facilities policies, taken together, help create an organizational climate. They determine whether (and which) members feel free to use the possibilities that are designed into their work settings. Some systems are very restricting in this regard, with few degrees of freedom, while others tend to encourage varied uses for their facilities. Within a given organization, some of the policies concerning use of facilities are very functional as far as allocating and maintaining resources; others are based primarily on the concerns or biases of one or more high-powered members. Usually there is a third batch of policies carried over from earlier periods when they may have made sense, but now they serve little purpose except to block full use of the facilities.

Formal facilities policies often tend to miss the mark for two main reasons: (1) the carryover of policies that have become obsolete or detrimental; and (2) the establishment of a blanket policy for a whole organization that, on the average, is appropriate for relatively few of the specific situations in which members of subunits of the organization must work. It would be helpful for leaders to keep both these points in mind and include in their management process some periodic reviews of their facilities policies in order to weed out obsolete or overgeneralized policies and institute needed ones that are missing. As a guideline for this process, it helps to aim for a set of policies that contains minimum rather than maximum constraints on members using their workplaces, and to remember that the point of physical facilities is to support users, not vice versa.

LOCAL RULES

Subunits in the organization also have a collection of more or less formal rules about the uses of their facilities. Divisions, departments, functional groups, and the like will set their own style to some extent, based on the nature of their tasks, the kinds of people involved, and the kinds of facilities they are using. For example, management groups who occupy space next to "dirty" processes (such as meat processing) tend to institute rules about who can and cannot come into the office area, or at least what condition their clothes have to be in. There may also be rules about where outsiders are allowed in a group's spaces or whether they are to be admitted at all. Sources of noise, such as personal radios, may be limited or banned altogether, and certain noisy equipment may only be run at specific times so as not to interfere with other nearby activities. There are sometimes rules about use of common areas and facilities such as lounges, seating areas, and cafeterias, while other groups leave this up to the individuals to decide for themselves.

Occasionally I have seen rules within a specific department about where people's workplaces can be located, based on their organizational status — near windows, in corners, on the interior, and so forth. These groups usually also have rules about what personal items can and cannot be brought into one's workplace. They may also limit the kind or amount of graphic display allowed in personal spaces (not that people always adhere to such rules — they sometimes violate them just to show that they feel the rules are an invasion of privacy). One of the most influential local rules concerns who can make changes in the facilities (or changes in the local rules, for that matter). This is often seen as the root of the real facilities management power in a given group — not what you *have*, but what you can *do* with what you have, and how you can limit or shape what others can do.

INFORMAL NORMS ABOUT USING FACILITIES

The third major component of influence on facilities use is the informal climate: the accumulated set of informal social norms about what people should and should not do in a given work setting. These are the unwritten rules of the game that "good" members must follow. Of course, work groups have norms about many aspects of work behavior besides the use of facilities, but those are not our concern here.

Local norms about facilities use can obviously cover many different topics, depending on the nature of the group and the design of the workplace itself. Some norms refer to specific items or setups in one's workplace, such as how furniture should be arranged (desk facing the door or facing a sound-absorbing panel); whether and what kinds of personal effects can be displayed (the norm may be that these should not be put up or that they should be and one who doesn't is being mysterious); the type and level of lighting, and whether lights should be on or off; whether an office door should be kept open or closed while the occupant is there; and if there are drapes over a glass interior wall, whether they should be kept open or closed.

Other norms are aimed at spatial behavior in the setting. Examples of this are how loudly or softly one should talk on the telephone or to people in the workplace; where papers, books, cups, coats, and so on should be stored when not being used; when one should say hello or acknowledge someone's presence, and when it is not necessary; when it is all right to enter someone's workspace (office or area) and when it is not; and who can use vacant offices, lounge spaces, or the like without being seen as overstepping bounds.

These are examples of the many kinds of possible spatial norms that members of a work group may enforce on one another. The feel of any particular group's workplace is determined to a significant degree not only by the design of that place but also by the mix and intensity of norms about spatial behavior. A group with norms covering many areas of layout and behavior would seem relatively tight and constricting to members, and it probably would be hard for them to be very adaptive to changing needs. They would continue to use their workplace in the same rather narrowly defined manner even if individual needs were changing. Conversely, a group with relatively few norms about space use would seem loose to members, and they would feel supported in experimenting or innovating with the things they did in (and to) their workplaces. Occasionally one finds a group that has a norm saying members *should* be innovative in the layout and use of their workplaces. Some design firms have this norm, since it is supposed to be an indicator of creativity in their business. Ironically, this climate can also feel constricting, if one is required to look innovative when he or she would prefer to be putting attention and energy elsewhere.

THE FEEL OF NEW WORKPLACES

The influences just described often come clearly into play when an organization creates and moves into a totally new work setting. This situation seems to call forth the maximum number of constraints on use, especially in the form of formal policies of both the organization as a whole and specific groups. I think leaders are influenced by a natural identification with the setting they have helped create. As a result, they want to keep it as near perfect as possible and do not want to see it go downhill quickly. Many kinds of "custodial" rules get generated as a part of the creation and move-in process, including most of those described above. Facilities-management group leaders are charged with keeping the new setting fresh and undegraded and with policing the occupants to make sure that they treat the facilities well.

The net result is that the organization's social climate often feels more constrained and stuffy in the new setting and the setting itself appears less flexible than the old one even though it may have many more changeable features purposely designed into it. People do not feel free to settle in, relax, and experiment with the new place. Consequently they feel less satisfied in the new place than they did in the old one, where rules became less important as it came close to the time to leave it. This attitude of discontent seems perverse to the leaders who created the new place, as if people are ungrateful for the wonderful things with which they have been provided.

This pattern could be called the "plastic on the furniture" syndrome, since it feels like those homes where tightly set up, formal rooms might as well be roped off for show because they have been declared "off-limits" to family members' everyday living activities. It is hard to feel at home in such a place, just as it is hard to feel comfortable in a work setting that appears to have as its main function being preserved forever in its brand new condition.

THE VALUE OF POLICIES AND NORMS

The general tone of this chapter may sound as if all rules, policies, and norms about use of work facilities are bad per se and should be eliminated. I do not think this is true, but the tone comes from my belief that in many organizations the system of formal and informal controls on use of facilities tends to be an evolutionary, unconscious combination of currently needed and outdated constraints whose cumulative effect is to be costly to users in terms of time, energy, and money. However, I do believe that some pattern of controls needs to exist in any organization. There needs to be some predictability about the kinds, amount, and quality of facilities that are needed and can be used by different groups. Rules are also needed so that competition for scarce resources can be handled without consuming an unreasonable amount of time and energy.

The problem develops when these control systems grow in an unconnected manner and take on surplus issues that do not need to be controlled (e.g., where the cost of allowing local option is small or nonexistent). As these controls evolve, the point of facilities management tends to be that of staying in control of maintaining facilities for their own sake, rather than for what is experienced or produced there by the users. Since the formal and informal controls build up over time, the cumulative impact is usually not recognized until the controls are thoroughly ensconced. Thus most organizations tend to end up with too many constraints about too many aspects of the use of their settings.

I believe that the most effective work environments are those where basic rules provide a structure or context for intelligent use of workplaces, but where there is also a commitment to make these the minimum constraints, leaving to the particular users the opportunity and ability to adapt the details of their workplaces and workplace behaviors to their own specific circumstances. The basic goal should be the support and stimulation of the users of workplaces, not the users' support of the workplaces. The latter is nice as an economical long-term pattern, but it is only truly economical if it is not at the expense of the former.

SUMMARY

As part of a commitment to a continuous process of workplace management, organizational and group leaders should assesss not only the adequacy of their facilities but also the appropriateness of the social-system controls that influence how well these facilities are being used. These controls include formal organizational policies, local subgroup policies, and informal group norms that prescribe the "correct" ways to use facilities. The accumulation of such prescriptions is a strong contributor to the overall climate of an organization and becomes particularly visible and pronounced when a new setting is created or an old one renovated.

Part II

PROCESSES FOR MAKING WORKPLACES

This part represents a significant shift in focus, from understanding the general patterns of organizational processes and their influence on space, toward suggesting how to influence and manage these ecological relationships to promote healthy individuals, groups, and organizations.

Part II has three goals. First, to present an overall approach to thinking about the processes of workplace design and management. Second, to clarify a number of these processes—the ones that typically tend to be fuzzy in the minds of leaders of American work organizations, yet are crucial to developing effective work settings. Third, to highlight a number of particular processes, problems, and issues that are usually overlooked or misinterpreted, in hopes that influential leaders or managers may deal more effectively with key choices and alternatives that may be assumed to be simple but often contain hidden options and costs. These three chapters are not meant to be a stand-alone formula for workplace design and management but to be combined with other technical experience and project management skills to help readers make conscious decisions about how to manage, alter, and design high-quality workplaces in their organizations. Chapter 5 will discuss the major issues and processes that affect the quality of ongoing facilities management. Chapters 6 and 7 will highlight what I believe to be the crucial factors in creating, occupying, and using new work settings in an effective manner.

Managing and Altering Existing Settings

I have already explained that workplace management should be a regular, continuous process containing regular points for testing the fit between users and settings, as well as regular mechanisms for making changes when misfits are diagnosed. In fact, a periodic assessment need not lead to a physical move to have been worthwhile; it may also lead to changes in the way the current setting is being used. In either case this is preferable to the hit-and-miss, crisis-oriented approach. In order for the space management process to be as natural as budgeting, performance reviews, production planning, and other recurring management tasks, there needs to be a strong norm in the organization's culture that says that managers should be and feel responsible for the effective design, use, and alteration of their own workplaces, as tools to greater system effectiveness.

THE MANAGER'S ROLE

There are a number of propositions that can be used to describe what I think managers should be responsible for, with respect to the facilities management process:

1. They should be measured and evaluated by their bosses on their effective and efficient use of physical facilities to accomplish their goals and those of the organization, just as they should be for use of other resources such as the salaries of the people who report to them.
2. They should establish a basic set of goals, values, and expectations for their own people about the use of physical settings and the handling of disagreements in this area.
3. They should develop (or cause to be developed) a model of how they want themselves and their group to do work, so that they will recognize

"pinches" when the setting is not helping them work in their preferred mode.

4. They should learn enough about the impact of physical settings on users so that they can evaluate the usefulness of their own areas in a competent, well-informed manner.
5. They should support their own people in shaping workplaces, experimenting, raising space-related issues, and contributing to the management of the common spaces that are not owned by any one group.
6. They should identify typical areas of conflict and disagreement in workplace design and management, and support their people in (a) working through these conflicts rather than avoiding them and (b) using these experiences to improve conflict resolution skills in other areas of work life as well.
7. As a group, managers should take the lead in defining an approach to spatial decision making and including the management of common, shared facilities.
8. They should from time to time create learning events (such as progress reports, group discussions, seminars, special guest lecturers) that are aimed at improving the environmental competence and spatial problem-solving skills of the people in their own groups (including themselves).[1]

GUIDING ASSUMPTIONS FOR ONGOING MANAGEMENT

Given the typical problems in workplace management and the role attributes I have recommended for managers, what should an ongoing facilities management process be like? The varieties of kinds of work organizations and changing situations make it inappropriate to tout any single management method as the right one to use, but as I pointed out in the Introduction there are a number of guiding assumptions that I believe flow directly from the ecological points of view expressed in this book so far. I see these assumptions as dealing with the most crucial aspects of workplace management, especially as an antidote to the ineffective management patterns described in Chapter 2.

---

[1]There are many methods for developing environmental competence. I discuss the process and problems in depth in "Defining and Developing Environmental Competence," in C. Alderfer and C. Cooper (eds.), *Advances in Experiential Social Processes*, Vol. 2 (Chichester, Eng.: John Wiley & Sons, 1980), ch. 9, pp. 225–44.

Overall Goals.   The overall goals for a facilities management process should be to promote a good match between users' needs and their facilities, to do this in an economically efficient manner, and to strive to create an environment that is alive and stimulating, not deadening and degrading. This assumption is critical, since its acceptance implies that productivity, cost, and climate are all important variables and that no one of them should drive out the other two criteria because it is easier to measure or identify.

Quality of Decision-Making Processes.   It is important in facilities management to use high-quality decision-making processes. Borrowing from the behavioral sciences, there are three main criteria that should be used to evaluate the quality of decisions (and the decision process):

1. *Technical quality.*   Does the decision solve the problem it was meant to solve, taking advantage of available knowledge, technology, and resources?
2. *Acceptance.*   Does the decision process promote a feeling of acceptance of a decision or solution in the users, and a sense of commitment in those who are expected to implement it?
3. *Impact on members.*   Is the decision arrived at through a process that enhances the sense of self-worth and competence of the people involved, or does it tend to lower their self-esteem by alienating them from real influence over their own immediate workplaces?

An effective facilities management process should reflect all three of these criteria when decision processes are instituted, and these criteria should be used to sort out problems when the decision process seems to be unsatisfactory to managers or members of their groups.

Minimum Constraints with Maximum Choice.   When establishing administrative rules and policies relating to facilities, we should strive for an overall effect of minimum necessary constraints and the maximum degree of personal choice consistent with maintaining a clear direction to the management process. As mentioned in Chapter 4, many management systems tend toward the opposite climate: a maximum of constraints as rules are laid on top of other rules over many years in an unplanned, untested manner. The two main areas where choice makes the most difference is in *personalization* of one's own work area and *spontaneous utilization* of facilities that have good features for the needs of the moment but may not be labeled as being for that particular use.

Support of Users' Experimentation.   These rules and the facilities managers should support users' attempts to adapt their settings to changing needs (rather than allowing the settings to become impediments as they become obsolete). Users' tinkering and experimentation should be encouraged as a positive act, rather than discouraged as an act of vandalism against the private property of the organization.

Encouragement of Feedback.   New feedback loops need to be built into the management process so that users can provide facilities managers with data about their actual experiences with their workplaces, as well as with the facilities management process itself. This is a fundamental assumption I make about any healthy management process. With feedback loops built in, it can never get too far out of alignment before it is corrected. In many organizations the opposite tends to be the case, and many signals are sent from the top leadership that people ought not to share their experiences (especially negative ones) with those responsible for facilities decisions, because it will be taken as complaining or having a "negative attitude."

Congruence with Other Organizational Values.   The environmental management process in an organization should be congruent with the values expressed by other management processes in that system. If an organization's leadership has been moving decision making toward more involvement of the members of various levels in decisions that affect them, then the workplace management process should also emphasize a participative approach. If, on the other hand, most management processes in the organization are relatively autocratic, with all decisions "owned" by the highest ranking person involved, then it is generally a waste of time, not to mention confusing, to promote participative decision processes in the facilitative management area. Too many signals and too much of the reward system tell people to defer to and be dependent on those in higher positions. Even well-intentioned attempts to share power in spatial decisions will be met with apathy, mistrust, or dependence, proving, in turn, to the higher levels that "those people" cannot handle such responsibilities (when it is really a predetermined outcome stemming from their whole style of management).

When looked at together, these assumptions describe a healthy, conscious approach to relating individuals and groups to their surrounding environments. Two questions readers might ask themselves at this point are (1) To what extent do I personally subscribe to this set of assumptions? and (2) How widely are these assumptions shared in my own organization and group? If the answer to either question is "very little," then clarifying your own assumptions or those of your group is a prior issue that should be worked on before trying to practice or evaluate very many of the other suggested methods that are presented in this and the following two chapters.

DIAGNOSING SYSTEMIC NEEDS

One way of ensuring that a number of the above assumptions are put into practice is to create some regular diagnostic processes for the ongoing management of the organization's facilities. The point is to do some diagnosing of physical facilities issues on a regular basis, not just when a move is being planned because space seems too tight. A *periodic programming process* is needed to identify system needs (at an organizational and/or subunit level), changes in needs, problems caused by facilities mismatched with these needs, and likely consequences if action is not taken to resolve such mismatches. The needs component should relate to your organization's identity, primary tasks, important historical forces that give it its physical shape, the economic climate in which it operates, and how its tasks and the social system designed to accomplish them are changing. This assessment will be developed in the next chapter.

Besides identifying your needs, you should build a regular data collection process to *assess how well they are being met.* This is best done on a periodic basis by designing the feedback loops already mentioned. Although many organizations tend to discourage feedback from users to decision makers (out of defensiveness or a lack of awareness of its importance), it is the key to a vigorous, ongoing facilities management process. A simple means for getting users' experiences should be designed into the decision process — make it clear *whom* they should tell about problems or ideas they have, *when* they should do it, and *what* will be done about it. The point is to get the data from real users and not just to work with the assumptions of high-power members who believe that they know the quality of others' experiences in the organization. They usually do not, mainly because their positions in the structure make it very unlikely that they could make many observations that would be useful in reevaluating the work setting.

The process I propose is similar to energy audits and retrofit processes for homes and other buildings in order to reduce fuel costs for heating and cooling. Since we are dealing here with human energy loss as well as physical energy, we should do audits and retrofits for the pattern of use of individual and group energy in an organization. These audits would lead to periodic "overhauls" or tightening of the facilities —

for a group, for common areas shared by groups, or for the organization as a total system.

THE ONGOING FACILITIES MANAGEMENT PROCESS

Periodic diagnosis will not lead to much change unless there is a healthy structure for the process of facilities management in general. Since there are many reasonable ways in which such management can be structured, I will present some ideas that can guide such a structuring process, including specific examples of ways that it could be done if you have certain goals in mind. The key is to have in place some social processes for doing maintenance, alterations, and tinkering with present facilities as they are used over time.

First, it is very important to develop a *long-range master plan* that lays out a general facilities strategy, expected growth rates, tradeoffs that are deemed by top management to be worth making, and the role relationships of various participants in the facilities management process. This plan does not have to be excruciatingly detailed, but it must be specific enough to provide a context for spatial decision making and maintenance decisions at different levels of the organization's hierarchy.

Second, there is a need for a *set of decision-making guidelines from top management* that identifies different types of facilities management issues and decision areas. These guidelines would roughly define (1) decisions that are local option and can be made almost unilaterally, (2) decisions whose impact cuts across group boundaries and therefore require coordination and the recognition of interdependence as a factor, and (3) decisions that affect the whole system and require top management approval because they potentially alter the pattern of organizational facilities or the options for future uses of those facilities.

Third, it is also useful if the organization's leaders provide a *set of budget guidelines* detailing the extent to which a manager must use his or her own budget for maintenance and alterations, as well as the circumstances under which it is possible to draw from general company funds (and for what purposes). These ballpark guidelines can save a lot of time and energy wasted in exploration of alternative layouts that have no chance of ever being implemented because they cannot be funded. It is better to know the guidelines early on and focus on those things that can be done.

Another necessary element that is often missing is *a visible conflict-resolution structure* for handling lingering disagreements. This should be part of a general process for managing common areas—lobbies, eating places, shared equipment spaces, lounges, exercise rooms, restrooms, and so forth. Rules should be established about how these areas should be managed and who influences decisions there.

The issue remains of how to structure the role of functions that are specifically tasked with maintaining and managing the organization's physical settings. These units may have various names: facilities management, administrative services, building administration, the maintenance department, and so on. Since my strong preference is for having line managers take responsibility for effective use of their own physical resources and jointly share responsibility for management of the physical patterns of the whole, this implies a particular flavor for the specialized facilities function, no matter what it is called. They should first and foremost be able to *work collaboratively* with the various user groups whose work lives they influence. They should think of themselves as trackers of use patterns and problems, facilitators of effective settings management and use, and implementors of decisions taken by user groups. They should not think of their primary role as that of owner of the facilities or as monitor acting as a surrogate for the top management owners. In either case, they should not adopt an air of sufferance — as if they are *allowing* the occupants to use the facilities as long as they are on their good behavior. Unfortunately, this is how facilities people are often encouraged to think of their role, since their performance seems to be measured on how little they spend and how little the setting requires alterations, not on how fully the setting is being used or how helpful they are being to the users. The maintenance *process* should be considered to be the joint responsibility of line managers and the maintenance group. The criteria or standards for maintenance, and at what costs, should be heavily influenced, if not set, by user groups' managers, and certainly not by the maintenance function unilaterally.

Case Example

To help clarify the points made above, I present a set of suggestions I made to a client system about how they might manage their corporate headquarters building in a way that involved users. The suggestions were grouped according to specific area of use.

For joint facilities on a given floor (conference rooms, copying center, coffee area, hallways, elevator, lobbies), there will be issues concerning scheduling, legitimate users, experimentation, alterations, decoration, expansion, and so on. One way to handle these would be to create revolving floor councils, with representation from each resident group on the floor plus someone from building administration. The committee would be publicized so that users would know to whom to go if they had complaints or ideas to improve the common facilities. The council would meet every two months or so to review use of current facilities, identify issues, and start actions to solve problems or pass them on to the right people to solve. A group's representative should be changed periodically, maybe once a year.

For building-wide facilities (cafeteria, elevators, mail service), a group made up of representatives from each floor council plus a building administration representative could be established. There should be a good mix of the various divisions' people in this group. It would meet less frequently than the floor councils to hear issues, identify problems, assign responsibilities, and track the degree of fit between users' needs and the building-wide services.

For the headquarters work environment as a whole, there needs to be a periodic review process to examine the fit between the work setting and the needs of the organization (both work needs and personal needs of members). Perhaps this could be done about every nine months by the division managers plus representatives from the floor councils and from building administration. This forum would also test whether the systems monitoring the joint facilities and building-wide facilities were working or needed alteration.

For individual group areas, the managers should establish some visible mechanisms for clearing and initiating space changes in their own areas. They should also inform the floor council about what they are doing so that the impact on the whole floor can be tracked.

For individuals' workplaces, people should have a clear, visible picture of whom to go to to get technical problems solved or implemented. They should also be supplied with some guidelines about what kinds of alterations to their workplaces would and would not be in keeping with the plan for the building as a whole.

MANAGING THE SOCIAL INFLUENCES
ON FACILITIES USE

The final issue I want to discuss in this chapter is the periodic need to diagnose the effectiveness of the rules, policies, and norms that have been developed to influence how members use and alter their settings. Since these form a major part of the climate or feel of the social setting, they need periodic testing and overhauling. Following the principle of complementarity, people's experiences result from a combination of social and physical settings; in some cases it turns out to be just as effective and much cheaper to change policies or norms than to make alterations in the organization's physical features.

As discussed in Chapter 4, the primary objective of facilities management should be to promote a climate of full use and innovation — to encourage people to do more with what they have. One aspect of this is to develop rules that encourage users to alter or experiment with structures and uses of physical structures. Another aspect is the strategy of using an existing setting for experimentation and alternative testing when a move to a totally new setting is being planned. The current site can be a sort of laboratory to generate relevant information to guide decisions about the new facilities, if this process is legitimized by top management. This experimentation can take many forms, such as changing traffic patterns, trying out new forms of task or ambient lighting, testing new furniture systems, or setting up a whole area in a new form of layout.

The energy required by alterations to large-scale existing settings can approach that required to create a new one. In some instances redoing an installation may be *more* complex than new construction at a new site, since you are having to work on large areas that are still being used. Therefore, many of the points in the next two chapters on creating new settings can be applied to major renovation projects as well.

CHAPTER 6

Defining and Structuring the Process for Creating New Settings

In this and the following chapter the focus will be on the planning, creation, and occupation of new work settings, such as an office building or factory/office complex. The discussion is divided into two roughly equal parts, defining the process (this chapter) and running the project (Chapter 7). I want to make clear that this is not meant to be a comprehensive step-by-step technical blueprint for how to run a design project and manage all the technical aspects of a building program. The emphasis here is on the organization as an ecological system, and especially on those organizational aspects of the planning, design, and moving process that I have observed to be typically the most difficult or elusive. Some of the activities that will be covered tend to be done poorly, others have specific organizational factors that work against them, and some are often overlooked altogether in the excitement and anxiety associated with trying to create a new workplace. All three conditions can reduce the effectiveness of a project unless they are recognized and dealt with in the design of the process as a whole.

The following discussion of the design process is structured according to the role responsibilities of different classes of organizational positions: top executives, middle managers, and professionals. I have considered their roles for various stages of the process, from first conception to post-move adjustments and evaluation.

THE ROLE OF THE TOP EXECUTIVES

Members at all levels of an organization have many useful roles to play in the creation of new workplaces. There is one role, however, that the top leaders of the system must take on themselves, even though they may delegate some of the initial details to others. This role is that of formulator of an overall view of the purposes, social structures, and project structure associated with the creation of the new setting. The organization's leaders should be responsible for defining these and managing them in an overall sense, since the outcomes affect the future shape and life of the whole system. I see them as responsible for five early stages of the process. There is no one else in the system who has the kind of crossboundary responsibilities implied by such a role.

Stage 1. The First Pass at Defining the Project

In defining the project, the leaders of the system should ask themselves a fundamental group of questions, including

- Why are we considering creating a new workplace? What is happening or will happen that makes this seem worth considering?
- What would we really be trying to accomplish? What should our goals be for such a project and how would we measure whether we had succeeded? (What indicators would we use?)
- What sort of history of workplace management do we have in our organization? What does this suggest about the approach we should take?
- What is our time frame? How great a sense of urgency or ease do we feel, and how would this affect the structure of the project?
- What are the specific problems we are trying to solve? If we did not use the solution of creating a new workplace, what are other alternatives that might also solve these problems? Are any of these significantly cheaper and worth developing as a serious alternative?

At this point it might be easier to visualize this earliest stage with a case example. I was asked by the executive group of an industrial concern (which I will call Consolidated, Inc.) to help them in the early stages of planning a new headquarters building. It was to house about 250 people and be located less than a city block from their current location, four leased floors in a six-story office building. I began by doing a small diagnosis of the members' reactions to their current workplace and submitted the following report.

Case Example: Consolidated, Inc. Having visited Consolidated several times and chatted with a fair number of people about how they see the current headquarters building, I thought it might be useful to summarize some of the main themes. This should help in setting goals and making choices about what to include and emphasize in the new building.

Almost without exception everyone mentioned *the lack of adequate temperature controls* as being a major drawback of the present setting. They feel the new building will be a failure if there is not a substantial improvement in this area. A number of people also spoke wistfully about wishing that they could have a window that actually opened — but they expect not to have this "luxury."

Many people mentioned the blandness of the current building: few plants, little use of color in any systematic way, almost no interesting graphics that give special identities to different areas. They also wondered why there are so few signs and graphics that tell one how to find individuals and groups.

Noise was mentioned by many as a problem with current space. Part of this is due to overcrowding, part to poor placement of noise generators like typewriters so that they project noise to the wrong spots. Noise control will be a big issue in the new layout, and needs to be carefully considered.

Many people mentioned *the lack of adequate places for informal contact*, taking breaks, eating lunch, and so forth. This is an obvious need in the new design. The same goes for careful design and location of other shared facilities such as coffee-making and copying facilities (whose locations are seen as inconvenient now). A few people said they wished there would be a cafeteria in the new building, so that Consolidated people could eat together, but they said it without much hope, it seemed.

One point was frequently raised: the headquarters is missing a key piece of design — *places for visitors or nonfull-time residents* to be when they are at Consolidated. There are almost no appropriate areas for visitors, company field people, consultants, contractors, and so on. This holds for both waiting spots and temporary working spots. The result is discomfort for them and for headquarters people who feel responsible for them and want to have the experience form a good impression of Consolidated. The theme that hit me is that the headquarters is definitely an "open system" with people moving in and out, but it is designed as if it were a closed system. This should be reversed in the new building.

Relative locations of people and departments were often mentioned as needing to be better thought out than at present. Locations were often described as random, accidental, or just expedient. The idea of having easier access to accounting than at present was popular with almost everyone. This is one of those functions that is often described as out of the mainstream, and yet many people have to have contact with it.

The programmers' area was described as an unequivocal disaster —

too dense, too noisy, poor layout, and too transient in terms of always shuffling people around. It would help to have their new area done especially well, and with their own inputs into the process early, rather than as an afterthought.

A number of clerical people said that they liked the idea of having a *less closed layout*, as long as it did not end up with big bullpens. They would like a balance (and so would I).

As far as *social climate* is concerned, several people said they hoped that the new building did not feel like a new house where you could not do anything for fear of messing it up. This reminds me of the relatively inhuman, autocratic feel of the bank building that we toured, with all their symbols of top-down control: no smoking; no lights that people can adjust for themselves; time clocks; no personal pictures, posters, or other human traces. I hope the new building does not generate this sort of climate — I do not think it fits Consolidated at all.

Most people said they know next to nothing about the new building and how it would take shape, and they hoped to hear more as time went on. This speaks to the need to design some regular communications activities so that the process feels like an open one, not closed and secretive.

There are obviously many other factors that should also be considered in the new design, but I thought it would be useful to put down what I was hearing from people, so that we would have these points as a check on how the design and process are developing.

One of the most important points I tried to remember and to advocate in this preliminary musing was to separate *problem* statements from *solution* statements. A problem statement would be, "We feel crowded and do not see ways to expand to meet our growth rate." A solution statement would be, "We need more space," which already assumes that the answer to feeling overcrowded is to obtain a larger facility. This preempts other possible solutions, such as reorganizing groups or work methods so as to use the present facilities differently. When solution statements are presented as the statement of a problem, they channel thinking away from truly diagnosing the problem, its causes, and criteria that would be used in comparing solutions, not to mention steering the preliminary thinking away from considering a variety of possible approaches or solutions.

After reviewing this report, we set up a two-day managers' workshop to develop their preliminary definition of the new building project. The discussion covered three broad areas: (1) the ways in which they define, organize, and evaluate their own work; (2) a comparison of these with the needs of the next few years, especially in light of a predicted downturn in the business climate; and (3) ways in which they could work better in relation to the new climate and restructure themselves physically. The workshop served partly as an educational experience about organizational ecology and partly as a work session that generated some preliminary criteria about the new place, especially ones relating to what it should feel like to the headquarters' employees. They followed this with a first pass at what the new facility should be like. This included broad statements or rough guesses about *size* or scale of the project; the *style* (visual and functional) the group wanted to project with the new building; *shape* — how the facility would be organized (vertical, horizontal, linear, circular) in terms of relative location of its different parts; the degree of importance of *options* — how much flexibility for future changes they thought should be built into the design; *technology* needs — that is, the main tasks that would be done in the new facility and what level of advanced or existing technology would be required to support these tasks; and *budget* — what level of investment would be appropriate and acceptable, very rough estimates of the costs of the kind of facility they are describing, ideas about how such an investment would be financed, and how long it would take to put together a financial package. One issue they did not consider was that of possible *locations* for the new headquarters building, since they were already committed to the new site because of a number of preceding events. They did review whether the commitment was firm and still made sense, just as location should be an issue for any executive group at this stage.

Leaving the case example, I want to be clear that dealing with location, size, style, shape, options, technology, and budget guesses in a first review is not meant to be the definitive program. This is simply a means of getting the executive group into the process so that they have something on which to base the other aspects of the design process, some sense of where they are going so they can create a structure and process to get there. Sharper definitions of the program itself will be discussed shortly in stages 3 and 4.

Stage 2. Structuring the New Workplace Project

For this next stage, the executive group should still be the main participants, jointly setting up and starting the process that will carry through the project from an idea to an accomplished, occupied reality. The future flow of the project is so affected by its beginning structure that the executive group as a whole should be involved in shaping this structure, so that they both understand it and are committed to doing what is necessary to support it. When such understanding and commitment are lacking, key executives can become nervous about events that are predictable and normal parts of a complex building project, and I have even seen such projects short circuited because they were perceived as being out of control.

The kinds of decisions or issues that should be addressed at this stage include the tasks to be done in order to get the project under way, managed, and completed; the different phases that the project will go through; rough timing estimates for how long each phase should take, how much they will overlap, and which tasks must be done early so as not to block later stages; and definitions of structure — who should manage various aspects of the project, and who should do the various tasks defined.

The point here is not to get seduced into trying to do all the work in a cursory fashion and make lots of detailed decisions, but to set up a structure in which the executives have confidence. It should define authority, expectations, and accountability in the framework of tasks, stages, and milestones that will give the executive group a means of sensing whether the process is on or off track. The actual features of such a structure will vary with the organization's situation and the cast of people involved.

The most elaborate process I have seen included the following elements: a program manager; a steering committee of executives that "owned" the project; regular planning and review events held by the steering committee; a facilities group to work with implementation of technical decisions; project managers for key subtasks (site development, human system changes, the move itself, and so on); crossdepartmental advisory teams to work on design issues for the building as a whole; functional and other groups (representing employees) who worked on more elemental design and layout problems; outside resources such as architects, space planners, engineers, contractors, and the like; regular project meetings combining client and contractor representatives; and a process-facilitation group to help in the collection and application of human system information (peoples' problems, preferences, wishes, and so on).

The actual mix of roles, groups, and events on a project will depend on the scope of the project, how other projects are typically handled in the organization, and the executive group's readiness to experiment with new forms of temporary structure in order to set a particular tone for the project. New elements may also be created at later stages to deal with particular issues or to flesh out activities better defined in stages 3, 4, and 5 (which follow). At this point what top management needs most is an image of how the program is to be accomplished so that they can commit people and monetary resources to that plan to make the best use of them in achieving a high-quality outcome.

This is also the point where a crucial choice is probably best made:

the selection of the primary designer or architect who is going to work with the project and give it a particular feel or style. If an architect is chosen before this point (as they often are), it is hard to know whether their particular approach and style will be compatible with the goals and feel desired by the executive group. If he or she is chosen much later, they miss out on opportunities to help shape some key pieces (such as the program or final site selection) that will constrain all the other steps in the project.[1]

Stage 3. Defining the Program

Stage 3 is the crucial step of defining the program in more detail. It is at this stage that the organization's leaders should specify the ecological content of the project — what the setting should be, what problems it should solve, and how it will contribute to fulfillment of the goals of the organization and its members. The participants in this definition process should probably be the top executive group plus other key players as specified by the overall program structure they have defined.

One of the most important aspects of the program definition is an analysis and description of the organization itself: its mission, goals, values, climate, myths, significant history, primary tasks, crucial aspects that are ripe for change, how the new place should support these change goals, and so on. What is the organization now, and what is it becoming? How is it likely to change over the life of the new facility, or even while the new facility is being built and occupied? This reflection on who they are and where they are going is a step that is often given short shrift in design projects, if it is done at all. To do it right requires a willingness to describe the organization and its members honestly, and to deal with issues that may have been left undiscussed and unresolved because key leaders have not wanted to face the disagreements that they would spark.

And yet, if this analysis is not done at the early stage of defining the program, two costly patterns can result. One is that the finished work setting may not be very useful for what the organization is becoming. The new facility will end up as more of a monument to the past because the design program represented historical myths more than current realities and future trends. The other pattern is one where the progress of the project is slowed down or stalled at various points where hidden disagree-

---

[1]For some thoughts on the timing of this selection (and a good summary of a new headquarters project) see Robert F. Gatje, "Building Your Dream Headquarters," *Across the Board* (November 1983): 28–33.

ments can no longer be avoided because concrete choices must be made that inevitably rule out other options or points of view. Such delays can be very costly in terms of person hours, schedule slippage, and even physical reworking of the structure.

I have found that one of the most useful things that a top group can do to generate a feel for their building program is to develop an overall theme — an image or metaphor for what they are trying to create physically and socially. The metaphor can be from any aspect of life, depending on what images seem to fit the executives' notions about the project: a high-rise apartment tower; a dense, highly centered medieval village; a strip development with services arranged in a linear fashion; a town square from nineteenth-century America; a factory for ideas and information; a campus or "think tank" setting. The important point is for the executives to share their ideas and fantasies early so that they can arrive at some agreed-upon image that helps them communicate what they want to the various design agents who will work with them. The absence of such an image or theme tends to produce a setting that may have high-quality parts but does not project a sense of wholeness or identity. (See Chapter 8 for a discussion of the ways in which the work setting can contribute to such a sense of organizational identity.)

Stage 4. Defining Classes of Decisions

This step could be a part of stage 3, but I want to draw particular attention to it because it often does not occur at all, at least not in any clear manner. The purpose is for the organizational leaders to identify different classes or types of decisions that need to be made for the building program and to state clearly who has the final authority to make those types of decisions.

In most organizations, there are three main types of facilities decisions classified by who is involved in them:

1. *Imperial decisions* — made by top executives with little consultation from other levels (since the executives believe they have good data, good criteria, and the right to make decisions unilaterally).
2. *Informed decisions* — made by top executives with a good bit of input from others.
3. *Participative decisions* — made by various members or groups in the system depending on the topic.

Imperial decisions, in my opinion, should be minimized because they are too prone to positional bias and distortion. Both imperial and informed decisions are made by top people because they feel they have both a right and a duty to decide certain matters, while other topics may lend themselves to the participation of different levels.

For example, there are large-scale decisions that affect the whole organization: the location of the new building, the overall assumptions about size, style, rough layout, and so on. These have been referred to as decisions related to the "shell" of the facility.[2] These decisions have a relatively long impact life (say forty years or more). It seems likely that the top executives would want to reserve for themselves such final decisions, even though they may ask for supporting information from those at other levels of the organization.

Next are types of decisions that fall into a middle range in terms of scope and time of impact — decisions about the "scenery" of the facility: stacking plans (who will be on which floors), decorative themes for common areas, particular materials and layouts for shared facilities, traffic-way patterns, and so on. In order to bring the most familiarity to bear on these decisions, they should presumably be "owned" by managers or groups that are most affected by them and care the most about the configurations that are created.

The final type are the decisions that relate to the props in individual and group workplaces: what Duffy, Cave, and Worthington call the "sets" in which people perform their day-to-day work roles, and which may be changed around fairly frequently as the users and users' needs change.[3] The goal here would usually be to have as many decisions as possible on details (specific furniture, arrangements, immediate decorations, work materials, and so on) made by those most affected by them, in the context of broader guidelines provided by top-level decisions about scenery and shell.

The idea, then, is to lay out a rough map of the classes of decisions and who should make them. There should also be some indication of the timing of decisions — when are they needed, and which have to precede or follow which. One of the trickiest problems is to make spatial decisions at the appropriate time — neither so late that other parts of the schedule are significantly delayed nor so early that the appropriate data that would help in making a good choice are not yet known. In my experience, anxiety about making decisions too slowly and hurting schedules leads to a pattern of making many decisions too early (and therefore poor-

[2]See Frank Duffy, Colin Cave, and John Worthington, *Planning Office Space* (New York: Nichols Publishing, 1976), 4–7.
[3]Ibid.

ly) on the assumption that every decision gotten out of the way is like money in the bank. If a decision is made too soon, you may have nothing banked except the hassle of undoing an obviously unworkable decision.

Having the top executives identify classes of decisions and who makes them eliminates ambiguity and allows the members to use their energy in useful ways. If the top members are clear and have agreed about which decisions they want to hold onto or control themselves, they also send clear signals to the lower levels of the organization about the areas for which they expect others to be influential and accountable. In the absence of this clarity, there is a tendency for everyone to play it safe and assume that the top executives own the whole project and any decisions they choose to pick out of the flow. People tend to defer and wait for direction from the top, even when there is little likelihood that it will come (the top members may not even know that others expect them to decide), and the whole process tends to be sluggish.

There are therefore three objectives to be achieved by mapping out a decision matrix:

1. By delegating influence and initiative at all levels of the system, many people can influence different aspects of the program and do this in an excited, forthcoming manner rather than as tentative, risky moves.
2. By seeking decisions based on high-quality information, the right inputs will go into decisions and result in informed choices (versus simply legitimized choices).
3. By giving people influence over those aspects of the project that affect them most directly, they will feel both ownership of the new setting and commitment to making it work when it is occupied.

Having the top executives identify which decisions to hold and which to delegate is particularly useful in the arena of workplace design, since the more concrete and visible the outcome of a decision process will be, the more executives tend to feel at risk in letting go and the more they tend to control the process. They feel they can be easily criticized if anything does not work, but ironically more things are likely not to work if they hold on too tightly than if they map out what to hold and what to delegate for others to decide.

Stage 5. Refining the Program and Structure

Having completed stages 1–4, the executive group then needs to make a serious review of both the building program as a whole and the social structures that will carry it out. The executive group and key program or project leaders should define, in more detail, aspects such as the overall goals of the program; the location, nature, and size of the facility to be built; the major organizational, behavioral, and task parameters that the new facility should support; the time schedules as they can now be estimated, including major milestones for checking the progress of the project; and overall budget figures, cost estimates, and financial guidelines that can be used by those who are expected to make the various types of decisions described in stage 4.

Taken together, then, stages 1–5 represent an integrated start-up sequence for a new building project. These steps all require the top leaders of the organization to involve themselves in activities that set the context within which people at many levels can contribute to the program. The leaders will then be involved to varying degrees depending on the processes they have defined and their own individual levels of interest in the program.

MANAGERS' ROLES IN THE PROCESS

So far this chapter has focused on what I believe are the essential early tasks that the top executives should do in order to provide effective leadership and direction in creating a new facility or complex. Having provided this overall direction, the next few levels of management are in a better position to play a number of different kinds of roles in the space planning process, and it would be useful to mention a few of these roles here. One is to serve as a sounding board to test the overall program and organizational diagnosis to see how well the diagnosis fits the users' experiences and whether the program will work from an ecological point of view. I have often seen major problems spotted when executives tested their notions on the managers below them. Probably the most important role that managers should play is taking the lead in the definition of the directions and environmental needs for their own areas of responsibility. An analysis for each area of their mission, goals, tasks, technological needs, and likely growth or changes is a necessary complement to the global analysis done by the top executive group. It is also important that this analysis represent the group's needs and directions, not just the personal view and preferences of the manager, assumed to represent everyone else by proclamation.

Managers in the middle levels can also be particularly useful by serving on crossdepartment review or steering groups, checking on progress in design and construction of facilities that are shared by different areas or functions. Such managers represent a sort of "owners' group" for those kinds of common facilities, taking part in forums that test whether or not the emerging setting is appropriate and matches the top executives' original goals. These managers also need to clarify which aspects of the design and the implementation of their new setting they want to reserve for their own decisions or approval, and which they want to delegate to members within their function. This is the same sorting process done by the top executives, and if it is not done by these middle managers the process again tends to stagnate.

Finally, I think that a subtle but valuable contribution of managers to the workplace creation process can be made in the dual roles of communicator and controller. Communicator means sending clear signals to one's subordinates about the importance of the design/creation program, as well as keeping people informed about those aspects to which the manager has access and his or her subordinates do not. The controller role means being willing to free-up subordinates' time and attention so that they can also make contributions to the creation process, either on task forces or in shaping their own individual workplaces. A manager who takes the initiative to enable subordinates to participate if they want to can be a big help to the overall process, even while not necessarily getting involved personally with many concrete tasks.

OTHER MEMBER ROLES: PARTICIPATIVE PROCESSES

It should be clear from the suggestions I have already made in this chapter that my basic bias is toward having people at all levels involved somehow in the process of creating a new work setting. This is not to say that everyone should be involved in everything or the same thing, of course. The key to a successful participative space planning process is for the leaders to clarify in their own minds the questions of participation in what, by whom, and to what ends. These questions should be answered very specifically, and the answers should be different for different classes of decision and steps in the process.

There are several issues to be considered in choosing a level of participation. How are other processes in the company managed? Would a participatory process be consistent with usual business, or would it be an experiment? Will people at different levels have the skills to fulfill their roles, or will some training be necessary in order for the process to go well? Are people eager and expecting to be involved, so that omitting them would generate resentment? Or are they concerned about other things and expecting that the top of the system will take care of all the place decisions and just let people know what is to be done? It is worth doing some scouting and data collection to answer these questions. If this is not done, top executives tend to answer them based on their own personal biases, which may or may not reflect the actual state of the organization.

In choosing a level of employee participation for different aspects of the workplace creation process, it is useful to keep in mind that there are both advantages and disadvantages to involving the ultimate users in the creation process. Advantages include getting the information and experiences of real users, helping people feel involved in a process that affects their daily work life, having them feel more committed to the outcome, and speeding up some decisions since they are not stalled by hidden disagreements or resentment of the process.

The most obvious disadvantages are that a highly participatory process generally takes more of people's time and energy, some training may be necessary, and the outcome in some areas of design, decoration, or layout may be different from the personal preferences of the top executives.

It seems to me that the advantages usually outweigh the disadvantages and represent a more vital mode of organizational functioning. But this is not always true, and the costs and gains are worth considering up front so that leaders become comfortable with a coherent strategy in the use of power and influence for spatial decision making. If the leaders have a clear strategy, then there are many different social structures or devices that can help make participation a reality rather than an empty mythical term: steering committees, task forces, crossgroup teams, design review panels, facilities groups tasked with supporting the user choice process, structured options for personal furniture or accessories, conflict resolution forums such as periodic review groups, and so on.

In the next chapter we will go into specific examples of some of these participative structures. I should mention here that one very important aspect of such structures is that they involve people who *really want to participate*. Dragooning people by telling them that they *will* participate has a long tradition in both military and business organizations, but it pretty much misses the point and neutralizes most of the possible advantages of a true participative process. Real volunteerism is a tremendous asset to such a process, and it is worth considerable effort to assign roles in the creation process to people who are actually interested and eager to be involved.

THE ROLE OF PROFESSIONALS

Although it is not my intent to deal in depth with the technical aspects of space planning and design as carried out by professionals in the field, a survey of the key roles played in creating a new workplace should at least mention the kinds of inputs and supports provided by professionals who may be either internal members or external resources to the organization. The success of a new workplace program is greatly affected by such professionals, and particularly by how well their contributions are integrated with and incorporate the inputs of the users themselves.

Internal Specialists

There will be a number of types of internal professionals who should be involved in the planning and creation of a new workplace: facilities managers, engineers, maintenance specialists, designers, and so on. The actual mix depends on how the organization is structured. From this chapter's earlier discussion, it should be clear that I do not think these professionals should just be handed the job of creating a new place and told to make it happen (as is sometimes done). Rather, I think that they should be included in the *planning process*, not just expected to execute the plans that have been made by others. If you choose a relatively participative approach involving user inputs and user work groups, the internal specialists should be taught and encouraged to work in this mode. The reward systems and performance measures should also be shaped so that the internal specialists do not feel that they will be penalized for relaxing some of the tight control that they tend to maintain over facilities design and use. Unfortunately, many projects are set up by top management with cost and schedule expectations for the professional groups that have not been integrated with the other aspirations for user involvement. This results in different vested interests and a feeling of conflict between facilities people and future users, rather than the two working in combination. The facilities people feel they will suffer unless they execute an economical, neat, tidy, timely project; the users' interests are best served by running a relevant, exciting, responsive project. Unless the executive group makes a special effort to be clear about their expectations for user involvement, these two sets of criteria will not overlap very much.

Another broad category of relevant internal specialists would be those with expertise in human systems and interaction: human resources, personnel, and organization development specialists. They can contribute through their knowledge of the organization, their skills in data collection and analysis, and their ability to design and run training events as needed (especially in a high participation project).

I make a point of these potential contributions because I have seen numerous instances where human-resources specialists with very valuable inputs to make have been left out of the design and creation process except when it related specifically to their own immediate work areas.

External Specialists

There will be many specialized technical resources that will be absolutely vital to getting a new workplace setting designed and built: real estate consultants, architects, engineers, space planners or programmers, interior designers, special facilities consultants (on telephones, information processing technology, office systems equipment, manufacturing technology), furniture systems suppliers and consultants, and so on. The most important point I want to make is that when selecting design professionals clients should use two broad criteria: (1) the nature and quality of their products, designs, and knowledge, and how well these match the program and identity of the organization; and (2) the *processes* they use in doing their work, compared with the process that the executive group wants to set up for the project. I have seen a number of poor matches between clients' goals and modes of working and those of the design people, and the gap could not be closed by good technical ideas.

Finally, I want to mention behavioral science consultants as useful external resources when an organization does not have this resource internally. They can help with either the content or the process of what the organization's leaders are trying to do. I have found that some of my most effective consultations have been in the earliest stages of a new building program, helping an executive group to conceptualize what they really want to do and to set up the process that they will use to get it done. This is probably the highest leverage use of consultation time, since it affects so much of what happens throughout the life of the program and the occupation of the new facilities.

SUMMARY

The top executive group has a number of stages in which it should be involved in creating a new workplace: roughly defining the project, structuring the project's process, defining the program, defining classes of decisions and who should make them, choosing design consultants, and refining the program and structure. The middle layers of management have key roles to play in testing the top group's program and process, providing data for their own areas, serving on crossdepartmental committees, communicating about the design process, and helping their subordinates make contributions. Other levels of employees can make valuable contributions if they are interested and if their inputs are truly wanted by the higher level managers. Technical resource people, both internal and external to the organization, are crucial to the project, and their selection should be based on both the content and the process (or style) of their work.

CHAPTER 7

Running and Completing the Program for New Settings

We now turn to some key issues in running and completing a successful program for creating a new facility. Rather than present a step-by-step blueprint, I want to highlight those activities that are not based on specific "hard" technologies (engineering, financial analysis) and so tend to be done relatively poorly because quantitative concerns drive out more qualitative ones.

EDUCATION AND TRAINING ACTIVITIES

We begin with education and training activities because they cut across all phases of a program and can be relevant for almost anyone involved at any hierarchical level. In my experience, most organizational building programs skip a number of important training steps. People are expected to fulfill certain roles in an area they do not deal with very often but are not helped to acquire the knowledge and points of view that would best support them in doing so. It seems to me that there are some regular questions for leaders to be asking throughout the design and implementation of the new building program: What training or educational activities will be needed, by whom, and at which points in the process? As an aid to answering such questions, the following is a summary of some education/training activities that would be supportive of a new building program and effective workplace management in general.

1. *Developing awareness of organizational dynamics and human systems concepts.* This is especially useful for the top executives to encourage thinking through of what they are trying to do and why. The focus is on understanding how the parts of an organization (departments,

hierarchical levels, and so on) relate to and affect one another, and how the organization interacts with its environment (see Chapter 12).

2. *Clarifying concepts in organizational ecology, such as the influence of environment on behavior and organizational dynamics* (the content of Parts I, III, and IV in this book). This is important for executives and managers who will be making decisions about overall design, locations, and layouts.

3. *Defining principles of layout design and types of furniture systems.* This activity supplies concrete information about good and bad ways to lay out work areas and defines the nature of different support systems to make them work. This is useful for middle managers and other members participating in the project.

4. *Fostering problem-spotting, problem-solving, and conflict resolution skills.* This is helpful for members and groups who will be diagnosing and dealing with problems and potentials of their own work settings.

5. *Developing positive attitudes and skills in environmental tinkering.* This would be an experiential program for users, to put them at ease and develop their skills at adapting and refining their own workplaces and group areas.

6. *Encouraging teamwork in space management.* This is a team building activity for managers and group members that emphasizes the issues, blocks, and methods for dealing with spatial issues where there is interdependence across group boundaries.

7. *Organizing a workshop on how a group uses its own setting and how it could or should use it.* This is important for groups from the top executive level down. It is an experiential activity in a group's own territory to heighten awareness of habit patterns and new possible modes of using the setting.

8. *Familiarizing the users with the features and special opportunities of the new building and its surroundings.* This is a basic orientation for all prospective occupants of the new setting, with a special emphasis given to supplying information that can help people adjust quickly and use the new setting well.

These examples are meant to be suggestive of the kinds of things that can be done to help people contribute in an informed, competent way to the processes of design creation and use of a new facility. Their aim is to avoid a situation where top executives delegate tasks for lower-level members without providing corresponding educational or training activities. The typically mixed results are then taken as evidence that the average member is either incapable or uninterested in making a good contribution to the creation of workplaces. If leaders *really* want the process to succeed, then they need to include the developmental inputs that will help to make this happen.[1]

DATA COLLECTION AND DIAGNOSTIC ACTIVITIES

A key variable that differentiates an effective new building program from an ineffective one is the degree to which high-impact decisions about location, geography, layout, relationships of parts to each other, and so on are based on current valid data about the nature and needs of the organization, its groups, and their members. Collecting such diagnostic data takes thought, energy, and time; it may loom as such an imposing task that it may seem simpler to avoid it and just proceed based on pooled impressions of the leaders who are guiding the program. And yet, a conscious attempt to define data needs and to lay out processes to get such data will pay back much more in terms of improved project quality and increased member acceptance than it costs. There is a (probably inevitable) tendency for top executives and middle managers to feel that they already know what the environmental problems, needs, and expectations are. This may or may not be true in a given instance, so the point is to create a process that will allow leaders to test and find out how good their senses of the needs are. If they are accurate, the executives have confirmed their views, and members know that this has been done (which generally makes them more willing to accept design solutions and try to make them work). If the executives are wrong, the data will challenge current perceptions and (if used well) improve the conception and design of the program, so that attention gets focused on the right issues and problems.

There are needs for data collection and diagnosis throughout a project: in the beginning to define problems and overall system needs, in the middle to assess needs and preferences of particular user groups in order to develop more detailed solutions, and at the end for a postproject evaluation of the effects of the new setting on the productivity and satisfaction of its users. Besides gathering data about the *content* (i.e., technical needs and problems), project leaders should also collect information about members' perceptions of the design *process* itself: How is it working and what might be done to improve or enrich it?

---

[1]For readers interested in exploring this issue in greater depth, I would suggest my chapter, "Defining and Developing Environmental Competence," in C. Alderfer and C. Cooper (eds.), *Advances in Experiential Social Processes*, Vol. 2 (Chichester, Eng.: John Wiley & Sons, 1980), ch. 9, pp. 225–44.

There are three main kinds of technical or "content" information that should be collected in order to guide a design project. One is a set of *programming data*: a definition of the tasks that are done throughout the organization, numbers of people involved, and physical-setting features that are required to support such tasks and people. A second is a compilation of the *personal preferences* of potential users of the new setting: what they see as their personal needs and desires for types of workspace, furniture, space, common facilities, decorations, and so forth. The third is a picture of the *interacting features of the human system*: how groups, individuals, and outside entities need to relate to each other in order to promote a healthy organization. Each of these three areas is important, but each provides only a partial diagnosis of the total needs to be met by the building program. For instance, it is important to know what people want in the way of a personal workplace, but by itself this leaves unanswered many questions about overall organizational geography and system-level needs for visibility and information sharing. An effective data collection process should be designed to be diverse and not exclusively focused on anyone's pet notion of the "real" data that count.

A detailed description of data collection methodology would not be appropriate here; there are usually professionals available within an organization who can help design and implement such processes. Human resources specialists can be useful for such a service, especially in the area of members' perceptions and preferences about workplaces. Professional space planners and programmers have their own well-developed techniques for collecting and analyzing data about tasks, work flow, and space requirements. The third area, concerning system dynamics and ecology, is more esoteric and there are fewer people who are equipped to collect and analyze this type of information. Some executives or managers could do this with appropriate training, as could outside organizational behavior consultants with an orientation to organizational ecology.

There remain a few other specific points that can help a building program be guided by the best information potentially available. One obvious point (often not observed in practice) is for the organization leaders and the project leaders to define clearly, early on, *what types* of data are most relevant and *from whom* they can and should be collected. Using the three broad categories just described helps to focus the diagnostic process and avoids the expectation that all pertinent data can come from any one group or source, be it top management, facilities managers, or user groups themselves. Each of these segments has useful information that can be collected and combined to facilitate good decision making for the project as a whole.

The next point concerns the *timing* of various data collection activities: When do we need this information (in terms of the sequence of steps in the project), and when can such information in fact be available to us? A frequent problem in this regard is the "decay" in usefulness of data collected and then just stored, especially those concerning user preferences and concerns. Doing an employee survey and using the results eighteen months later (which can easily happen in a long building program) looks like it will lead to user-oriented decisions, but the decisions may not reflect actual user preferences since there will be changes in situations, attitudes, and the employees themselves. At the very least some sort of check should be done to test the validity of the information close to the time it will be used. Collecting user information once and then staying with it will usually result in a program and decisions that are out of touch with the true state of the system, and they will be perceived that way by the members.

In addition, there are some kinds of information that really cannot be collected unless a prior step is taken. A simple example is the collection of people's preferences for the amount, type, and style of office furniture for their personal workplaces. People's views on this are very much limited by their previous experiences, and it is hard to know how to use the information obtained by just asking people what they would like. A much richer pattern emerges if some educational activities precede such a survey, so that people get a chance to see and experiment with a variety of current furniture alternatives (guided by overall budget considerations), rather than just choosing from what they have happened to see or use in the past.

It should be mentioned that the kinds of information that can be useful in a new building program are quite varied: preferences for furniture; preferences for layout of personal and group spaces; likes and dislikes about existing workplaces; typical contact patterns with individuals by hour, day, week, month; attitudes toward different decorative styles; personal work styles and how physical workplace elements help or hinder them; and social norms or organizational policies that are seen as helping or hindering the use of one's work settings.

The final issue is that of *interpretation* of the data. It is important to know what data tell you and what they do not. For example, knowing that work flows happen a certain way and contacts between two groups occur with a certain frequency does not tell you whether they *should* happen this way (and therefore whether the new workplace should be designed to support such patterns or change them). That is a diagnostic question based on your model of where the organization is going and what a healthy mode of working means for it. Similarly, knowing what people say they prefer also does not tell you whether that is what should be done — there may be other systemic needs that are also crucial to the success or survival of the overall system. What it can demonstrate is that personal preferences and systemic needs appear to be in conflict, so that some integrative solution can be sought rather than just choosing one or the other as the single right criterion.

DEFINING PROBLEMS AND DEVELOPING SOLUTIONS

The middle phase of a new workplace project involves fleshing out and implementing plans for the many parts that must come together to make a coherent whole. I will emphasize some key aspects of this phase and provide some examples of how certain issues can be handled.

There are many concrete tasks to be done during this phase, such as defining needs in more detail for specific groups' areas and for the building's common areas; exploring currently available technologies that may be applicable to various problems such as communication, storage of information and materials, information processing, and so on; generating likely alternatives and ranking them as solutions to these problems; choosing and recommending solutions; laying out specific features and an overall plan for how the facility will actually get built; contracting for the jobs to be done and scheduling the various elements so that they fit into an integrated sequence; and periodically testing solutions on leaders, managers, and user groups as the solutions become crystallized.

These processes are helped immensely by the services and guidance of a strong external design team, especially if this team also understands human organizational issues as well as physical design problems. They can also assist in designing an iterative process that solves successively more detailed classes of problems, based on the overall program or framework. In my opinion, the design team's contributions get used best if they are combined with detailed work done by volunteer members of various user groups within the organization. Such members can provide a real service to the design process by defining, exploring, and choosing practical alternatives for different classes of design elements or issues.

A good way to visualize the possibilities of such volunteer user groups is to consider the structure developed by a client of mine involved in creating a major extension to their headquarters. The project manager set up five working committees, each of which was assigned one of five broad areas.

1. *Layout.* This group dealt with larger system issues such as which groups should be adjacent to each other, where common facilities (copying, food service) should be located, and the like. They worked on stacking plans (which groups would occupy which floors); space allocations by function; and size, number, and location of conference spaces. They also considered entrances and exits, foot and vehicular traffic patterns, and parking concerns. In other words, they considered the major macro-design choices that cut across group boundaries.
2. *Design.* This committee considered the macro-design level of specific elements within the overall layout structure. They articulated the "feel" the new place should have, as well as the specific elements that would generate such a feel: furniture, lighting, colors, materials, graphic design and use of signs, floor treatments, and so on. (This group had to stay in close touch with what the layout committee was doing.)
3. *Services.* This group collected information and defined needs and approaches relating to all the support services that the new workplace should provide in an efficient and effective manner. They worked on communications internal and external to the system (telephone, TELEX, mail, electronic mail, and so on). They defined levels of use expected for copying and information storage, and defined systems to handle these. They considered future management of the physical setting: building maintenance, trouble shooting, and security management. They also projected present and future needs for computational equipment (space, terminals, and so on), and worked on basic environmental controls for the computer areas and the building as a whole.
4. *Project implementation.* This committee concerned itself with the more technical sides of the project and was made up of volunteers who had previous experience in this process. They helped with liaison with contractors, architects, and local government agencies. They tracked the acquisition of all permits and supported the financial management of the project.
5. *Communications.* This group's task was to facilitate the overall communications process during the life of the building project. They identified information that should be shared about the project, as well as information gathered, from various groups and levels in the organization. They provided periodic building progress reports, set up a hot line for quick information, planned the basic move-in process along with project implementation, and helped design educational activities including orientations to the new building.

Each of these committees was typically composed of seven to ten members representing a cross section of the groups that would be occupying the new building. They defined problems and tasks, analyzed problems, explored alternatives, and selected preferred plans for their committees' areas. They did a lot of the nitty-gritty work that often gets loaded onto one small project team, and the members of the committees also served as contacts back to their own functional groups. They reported regularly to the project manager and occasionally to a review group made up of the heads of each committee plus the project manager. They held a large half-day event (actually done in two sections because of large numbers) for all users of headquarters buildings where the work of each committee was presented. Each committee designed and made its own presentation, and members with no previous public-speaking experience suddenly became quite visible and prominent, which enhanced everyone's sense of accomplishment.

The activity levels of the different committees went up and down with the various phases of the project. The first three — layout, design, and services — tended to be very busy toward the beginning, while project implementation and communications naturally had a steady work load throughout the project.

For another organization setting up such a process, the actual breakdown of responsibility areas might be similar to this one or somewhat different. It should presumably depend on the resources and interests of the members, the special design needs of the system, and possibly past problem areas that top leaders feel warrant especially close attention. However the division of effort is made, members of the committees should be helped in their work by facilities management people and the designers who are being used (and who will presumably use much of the committees' outputs). The committees should also be encouraged to pay attention to the issue of optimal timing for various classes of decisions — as was mentioned earlier — neither making decisions too slowly so that they back up the schedule nor too early when there is not adequate information.

One point to reemphasize about this middle working phase is the need to test out proposed directions and solutions as you go along, both with the top leaders of the organization and with the lower levels. This could be done by reporting periodically to one or more steering groups. The purpose is to avoid big surprises that are revealed when it is too late for anything to be done about them (if the solutions are received very negatively) without expensive rework and/or schedule slippage.

OVERSEEING THE ACTUAL CONSTRUCTION WORK

This is a phase of the program when you definitely need professional direction. There is no substitute for strong engineering experience directing the project on behalf of the organization. Project implementation

manager is not a role for amateurs, unless the leaders are willing to accept surprises, uncertain outcomes, rework, high costs, and so on. There
are many ticklish stages that need guidance and monitoring, and technical
experience in construction projects helps a manager know when to get
nervous and when to relax, when to step in and when not to get in the
way. One area in which such technical people can sometimes benefit from
other resources is in the area of *relationship management*, that is, of
handling their relationships with contractors, user groups, and power
figures in the organizational hierarchy. Project implementation managers
tend to be caught in the middle, squeezed by pressures from within and
from outside the organization. They are usually weaker in conflict man-
agement/resolution skills as compared with their technical knowledge.
One approach that I have seen work well is the designation of a pair of
implementation managers as co-project leaders: a construction-oriented
technical manager and a human-process-oriented organization development specialist.

COMMUNICATION PROCESSES

Communication helps to hold a new building program together
through the early, middle, and late stages. By seeking and sharing information in a timely manner, various constituencies (from top leaders on
down) have a sense of what is going on and where (if at all) their own
interests are being considered. If the flow of information is handled well,
people at all levels will feel involved and cared for. They also feel that
they have had opportunities to voice their concerns while things are being developed, not long after the fact.

When we talk about communication, what does this actually mean
— communication about what? There are a number of major classes of
information that need to be shared by the project leaders with organizational members on a more or less regular basis:

- The basic decision to create a new setting and the factors and reason-
ing that went into it.
- The planning process and building program: how it is structured, who
are playing various roles, and who people should contact if they are
interested in getting involved in the process.
- Basic assumptions about the schedule, timing of the phases of the program, organizational needs and directions, degrees of desired participation in different stages, and what the working groups are producing.
- Choices and options that are open and how people can influence them
(at different scales — big issues, medium-level, and as specific as one's
own desk and chair).

- What specific design choices will mean to the individuals and groups affected by them.
- Information about the moving and post-moving periods.

There are many media that can be used to communicate these kinds of information to organizational members: regular bulletins or newsletters; occasional update memos; periodic slide or film presentations; communication events such as public forums where committees' work is presented and discussed; managers' briefings to their groups, after having been briefed themselves; and so on. One of the chief tasks of the communication committee mentioned above would be to consider the overall pattern of communication needed: content, form, and media used, and frequency or timing.

Doing this well requires a fundamental attitude on the part of the top leaders who control the project and the project manager who shapes it day-to-day and week-to-week. This attitude is that "the facts are friendly" and it is therefore a good thing for people to know what is going on. If the key leaders do not feel that this is true, then there is no point in doing more than the bare minimum of information sharing. Doing it well takes time and energy and may generate issues and conflicts, but this is part of the real value since it provides a reality test on what is being developed. If leaders feel that such issues are a problem that should be avoided, then they are not committed to a visible design process and should not try to look as though they are encouraging participation in the project. A grudging communication process always shows itself for what it is and often gives a somewhat sour smell to the whole project. No matter how it is done, the communication process contributes to the shaping of people's expectations and attitudes about the new workplace. How people will feel about it once they are in residence will not be just a function of the design, but also of how it was created and especially of what they know about how it was created. People's perceptions are the key here, plus how these perceptions make them feel about themselves in relation to the new setting— whether they identify with it, feel ownership in it, feel free to really use it, and are committed to trying to make it work for them as best they can.

THE MOVING PROCESS ITSELF

Expectations for and reactions to the new setting are also influenced by the design and execution of the moving-in process. This needs to be treated as an important, designed event with a consciously orchestrated feel and shape to it. The organization's leaders should take responsibility for the move and at least set criteria for how they want it to be handled. They should not delegate the total responsibility for the move to lower-level groups, even though such groups will do most of the detailed planning and implementation. The top executives should know what is happening with this process, mainly because it sows the seeds for people's early experiences in the new setting by being their first concrete experience there.

An important task in designing the moving-in process is to include activities that establish realistic expectations about the move itself. People should know that it requires a coordinated plan, will take time and energy, and to some extent will be an inconvenience no matter how well it is done. Anyone who has ever moved their family from one home to another will know this is true. You should realize that not everything will go smoothly and work instantaneously. There will be glitches, some of which are unavoidable because they are unpredictable. This should be expected as part of the normal experience of moving a complex human system to a new location, not as an unnatural result of a bad design.

On the other hand, a careful job of planning the multitude of details of the move can help eliminate the avoidable glitches. It is particularly helpful for the group planning the move to run through some concrete trial scenarios, going through the process visualizing each step, who does the main work and who supports it, and what each of the user groups will be asked to do and when. This trial run is most useful if the scenarios are shared with user group management to test the impact of the plans on the groups: will they work for the transition? Another key element is to take an inventory of essential services that need to be in place in the new building before anyone moves in, and to decide which services have to be maintained in the old building or can be stopped quickly once a significant portion of the residents have moved out.

There may be particular pairings of groups that should be moved together since so much of their work depends on close contact between the groups. This possibility is part of the more general issue of what strategy to use for the moving-in process. Should it be done in shifts, spreading it over some period of time such as a week or a month, as parts of the building become ready for occupation, or should the total move be done in as concentrated a period of time as is physically possible? Many people with whom I have worked prefer the concentrated, one-shot move, but each mode has its advantages and disadvantages. Which one is chosen should depend on factors such as the nature of the system's work (can it be done while split in two locations), the schedule for finishing the building, the distance between the two buildings (the greater the distance, the greater the cost of a slow move), whether the organization's work load is heavy or light, and financial arrangements (e.g., what it costs to maintain a presence in the old building or to get into the new building early).

The other major component of the design of the moving-in process is the planning of what advance information to provide the people who are moving. There are several topics that seem essential. If the move is to a different location, there should be information about the new area: what services are available, points of interest, and travel alternatives for getting there. Design features of the new building and the assumptions on which they are based should be shared, as well as the key differences between the new environment and the old one that people are currently occupying. Major policies relating to security, access, and use of the new building should be communicated along with the names of groups or individuals whom people should contact if they have problems in the new place.

There are different ways in which such information might be communicated, such as newsletters, announcements, general meetings, planned tours of the new site and building, and a building information center that people can call or visit if they are curious or have questions. One of the best efforts I have seen in this area was a well-designed booklet describing the location, building design, internal layout (they were changing from a closed office layout to a modified open plan), behavioral issues and principles in using the new layout, and a whole battery of information about services and sources of further information or help. This booklet was prepared by members of the external design team and made a very favorable impression on the members.

THE POST-MOVE ADJUSTMENT PERIOD

The final, crucial phase of the new building program is one that often receives too little conscious design. It is the period immediately following the move, when people are settling in and getting firsthand experience with their new workplaces. There are several aspects of this phase that deserve special attention, especially since these early experiences can form relatively permanent attitudes and images in users' minds about how well they like and can use the setting. One aspect is the advance information that is shared by program management about how this running-in phase is likely to go. People should be clearly advised to expect that there can be many kinds of problems with their own work spots (intrusive lines of sight, noise problems, temperature variations, furniture features that do not work right), with group areas (some confusing or missing signs, carpet problems, equipment problems in meeting rooms), and with building-wide systems such as telephones, elevators, copying facilities, the layout of food services, storage, parking access, and so on. All these features may require adjustments once they start being used.

If people are prepared to expect this adjustment situation, they will be ready to do their parts. But in many moves they believe (or are led to believe) that everything will be close to perfect as soon as the move to the new building is completed. This will not be so and cannot be, so the issue is whether they are ready for problems and treat them as normal or as confirmation of their suspicion that the building was a bad idea or poorly planned and executed.

This period helps set the tone for users' attitudes and feelings about the new place and what work life will be for them within it. To help this be a positive attitude, the planning group needs to create a special social structure that will be responsive to all the major and small problems that the occupants will encounter while adjusting to the new building. This structure is also needed to offset the natural tendency of those connected with the project (facilities group, project teams, task forces, top executives who made the initial decisions) to feel defensive about any mistakes and omissions. This feeling leads them to be slow or testy in responding to users' problems, which communicates to users that they are primarily seen as ungrateful gripers. Conversely, the message that should be sent during this crucial period is that the project managers want to hear about all the problems so that adjustments can be made quickly.

The best design of such a post-move phase that I have seen included a hot line number for employees to call to register their problems, with a commitment from the move manager that there would be response within forty-eight hours — either a solution to the problem or a clear statement about what would be done and how long it would take to solve it. (In a very few instances the response was that the condition was built into the new setting and either had to be lived with or could be used as justification for changing the person's workplace if it was incompatible with their task needs or work style.) This trouble shooting was done by a two-person team: the facilities project manager and the lead designer from the external design firm. They also put out a weekly status report on issues, problems, and what had been (or was being) done. They created a structure to treat these adjustments as *business as usual*, part of the designed project scenario, not as a struggle of wills between hard-working facilities people and ungrateful occupants.

The tinkering phase should be planned for a period of time (say two to three months), which should be followed by a planned follow-up evaluation on aspects such as impact of overall design, user satisfaction, layout impact, norms and patterns of use, support-systems performance, and so on. In other words a reading should be taken of the ecological impact of the new workplace. Some specific sensing sessions may also be held with various groups on how the setting is being used, compared with its potential. Are the possibilities for efficient use being realized, and, if not, are the blocks to this physical or social? There is also a more general need to do periodic evaluations of the adequacy of the setting for users' needs, so that there is reinforcement of the notion of workplace management being a continuous rather than intermittent concern. Regular evaluations also help people (planners, managers, users) to learn about organizational ecology, what affects it, and how it affects them.

One last point about the post-move period: I believe that the project team should provide encouragement and support for people to quickly personalize their own workspaces once they are in them — *if* that is a value that is expressed by the management as a desirable feature of members' organizational lives. Clear messages should be sent that this personalization is permissible, so that people do not feel that it requires taking a risk. Some will do it and some will not, but both types will feel that they had the option to do it if they so desired, so the new location will feel more like it is really theirs. One way of making this support even more real is to arrange for a designer to be available to consult with individuals or groups about alternative steps they might consider in making their workplaces really feel like home to them.

SUMMARY

This chapter has been concerned with several of the key activities in running and completing a new workplace design program. These activities include education and training events, collecting and analyzing information, defining problems and developing solutions, overseeing the technical aspects of the project, developing effective communication processes about the project, designing the move itself, and structuring an effective post-move tinkering process. An example was presented of a new building project with a heavy user participation component, built around five working committees. In general the theme has been that the more future users are involved in the development of a new setting, the more likely they are to feel ownership and to share responsibility for making it work well. This commitment can be further enhanced by designing a post-move tinkering phase that is visibly responsive to users' inevitable settling-in problems, so that the users get an even stronger sense that their problems are important and worth being listened to and solved. A new work setting is a complex system, and it is a great advantage to have planners, designers, and users all working toward making it serve its purposes well.

Part III

THE ECOLOGICAL IMPACT OF WORK SETTINGS

The seven chapters in this part deal with the concept of organizational ecology, describing the main effects of work settings on their users and on the organizations to which they belong. By way of introduction, I would like to make some essential points about underlying assumptions concerning the ways in which settings affect users.

First, a particular setting generally does not *make* people do things; it provides a context in which it is easier or more difficult for actions to be taken. An office layout with seven private offices separated by long corridors does not require that the occupants not interact with each other; it just makes it less likely that they will do so.

Second, this effect is one of probabilistic influence. On the average, the probability of regular contact among office occupants tends to be lower in the linear, closed-door layout than it would be if they all could see each other even when in their individual workplaces. In other words, the impact of the setting is greatest on the *pattern* of people's experiences over time: on contacts, movements, activities that they will naturally tend to do versus those that require a special effort to do. Rather than controlling specific events, the largest effects of a setting tend to be in the *cumulative* impact on patterns of work and interaction over time. People who tell each other that there will be no change in their relationship because one person's office is being moved from right next door to the next building (or upstairs to the next floor) are sincere when they say it, but they usually find that the pattern of their contacts changes no matter how strong their intentions to keep it the same.

Finally, there are some cases where the setting is such that some things must be done there or cannot be done there. These tend to be fairly obvious, such as it being impossible to have an effective conference room set up next to a drill press on the shop floor. These are important factors to be considered when evaluating the impact of your settings, but most of the effects are more subtle, affecting the pattern of actions, feelings, and experiences over time.

With that background, we are still left with a selection problem, since there are a large number of ways one could look at the effects of settings. My main guiding principle for work with clients has been to select those areas of influence that I think have the largest cumulative impact on either individual users or the functioning of the whole social system. As noted, this impact may not be particularly obvious at any given moment, but the pattern revealed over time will be an important factor in shaping users' feelings, perceptions, actions, and accomplishments.[1]

The seven areas of effect that I will describe in this part include a sense of identity and ownership, social interaction, energy levels and vitality, task effectiveness, power and influence dynamics, boundary relations, and organizational climate. They were chosen because I believe they have a considerable (but often overlooked) impact on an organization's effectiveness and the feel of work life within it.

---

[1]For readers interested in the phenomenon of "place experience," I would recommend two books: Fritz Steele, *The Sense of Place* (Boston, Mass.: CBI Publishing Co., 1981) and Yi-Fu Tuan, *Space and Place* (Bloomington, Minn.: University of Minnesota Press, 1977).

CHAPTER 8

Generating a Sense
of Identity and Ownership

In this chapter I will discuss the ways work settings affect people's sense of identity and feelings of personal ownership of their day-to-day workplaces.

WHAT IS A SENSE OF IDENTITY?

In discussing the impact of settings on sense of identity, I will apply the term on three human levels: individuals, groups, and the organization as a whole.

For Individuals

A person's sense of identity is a mixture of awareness and acceptance. First, there is the awareness of who one is in a fundamental sense: strengths, weaknesses, likes, dislikes, pivotal values, skills, historical roots, associations with others (and who they tend to be), developmental directions, and so on. Second is the acceptance and valuing of these aspects of oneself: being curious about knowing oneself and basically liking whatever mixture of characteristics exists (versus trying to pick and choose, denying those aspects that do not fit some idealized image of what people should be). Personal "style" is another way of looking at this sense of identity — what and how a person does whatever he or she does.

For Groups

Since groups have no brain or heart, they do not really think, see, or feel anything. A sense of identity for a group is really a question of whether the members have a set of common, shared images of the group and themselves within it: who they are as individuals, common styles (if any, or the group's identity as a totally mixed group), the reasons for the group's existence (mission and goals), who are members and who are not, key social norms (informal rules) to which members adhere, key shared values, important elements of the group's environment, and possibly common aspirations for group development. If this sense of identity is well developed, the group will have a strong "feel" to it and nonmembers will tend to be aware of its distinct group style or culture.

For the Organization as a Whole

Just as for groups, it is tricky referring to an organization's sense of identity since it is not a living entity and therefore cannot sense anything. It is composed of members, however, and they all have images in their minds of what the organization stands for and how it feels to be a member of it. We can therefore think of an organization's sense of identity being defined by the awareness of its members of the system as a whole and their place within it: mission, goals, plans for the future, structure, common problems, strengths and weaknesses, typical relations with the surrounding environment and community, and so on. If this sense of organizational identity is well developed internally, it also tends to be visible to outsiders who have a sense of what it stands for, its mission, and the style of its members and groups as they go about their business.

Consequences of a Strong Sense of Identity

The next obvious question is, so what? Why does sense of identity make enough difference to include it as one of my seven areas of ecological impact dimensions? There are a number of consequences of a strong sense of identity that help define some aspects of healthy people and groups. For instance, people who have a strong sense of identity tend to make good choices about how they spend their time and energy, as well as with whom. They are "centered" in that they have a context for relating the various aspects of their lives to a central stream or direction. They tend to communicate who they are to others, so that others' responses to them are appropriate to their needs and intentions. They feel a sense of connection between themselves and their environment.

Groups and organizations with a strong identity draw to them people who are seeking such a setting in which to work. They also generate a sense of organizational excitement, since members sense the potential accomplishments that go with a system where people's energies are by and large focused and directed toward common goals rather than dissipated in dozens of compromise efforts brought about by the existence of many different styles and factions. (Energy and excitement are discussed specifically in Chapter 10.) If the identity of the system is projected to the outside world, more excitement is generated in organizations and groups that relate to the high-identity organization, since they can see what it stands for and how it can play a part in relation to themselves.

In general, a clear sense of identity is a factor that provides a context for action — for good choices among alternative paths and for focusing energy and attention in efforts that will add up to something rather than cancel each other out.

HOW DO SETTINGS BUILD A SENSE OF IDENTITY?

To illustrate the impact of settings on one's sense of identity, we will look at some examples from individuals' workplaces, group areas, and the organization as a whole.

One's Own Workplace

The most immediate setting where people can express themselves in physical choices and in turn be affected by being around those choices day-to-day is the personal workplace — office, work station, desk, or whatever. For everyone who has a more or less regular spot where they spend their work time, there are opportunities to influence that spot in ways that communicate information to both themselves and others about who they are as individuals. The simplest aspect of this communication may be the presence or absence of choices regarding colors; personal artifacts such as pictures, mementos, sayings or cartoons that have struck one's fancy; and the like. If there are no visible influences of the person on the workplace, the person may reject it as not really them, as simply a spot in which to be a transient — like staying in a room at some anonymous motel. The person may come to feel that the absence of traces of personal influence on their workplace is symbolic of an oppressive climate in their organization. If this is the case, then they also usually come to feel that it is a statement about their own identity as well (e.g., "I am a low-power person who doesn't have the right to do what I want with my own workplace," or, if the constraints come from within rather than from outside the person, "I don't have the ingenuity, initiative, or interest to think of special things that express myself in my workplace").

When people do personalize their workplaces, there are many potential ways in which these actions help sharpen their sense of who they are. Pictures and mementos say something about the social network with which they are connected (family, friends, work associates, celebrities with whom they have worked and been photographed, and so on). The choices of what furniture to have and how to arrange it form images of how they work and how they want to relate to those who come to visit, such as having a place to sit versus not having one, having one's chair protected from visitors by a desk, having places to do work while standing or just while sitting, and so on. I heard of an executive who had no seating places at all in his office, expressing his sense of himself as a man of action, always "on the go," as well as his expectation that visitors would be the same so as not to waste his time by camping out for long periods in his space.

One's willingness to change the look or location of his or her workplace is an indicator of that person's comfort with change or relative fixedness. The location of that workplace in relation to other people and activities is a constant message about where one is located in the social system of the organization. The sheer "elaborateness" of the personal influences in the workplace may well be an expression of the extent to which the occupant is a "place person" — someone who is inherently interested in the sense of place as an experience, and therefore likely to care about the nature of a workplace enough to influence it.[1]

When we visit a person's workplace, making inferences about what it "says" about him or her can be done with the above points in mind, but it is a tricky business. In order to read a setting for clues about a person's identity, we need to also know how it got that way. Does it represent choices made by the occupant or by someone else who decided what that workplace should be like? If the influences were done by the occupant, do they reflect various interests, modes of working, and modes of relating that are really those of the occupant, or do they represent an idealized image of what he or she would *like* to be, expressed by conforming to some model of what the "right" workplace should look like? It is often hard to tell whether a workplace is expressive of real or idealized images without knowing more about the person. One clue that it is an idealized identity comes if the occupant seems often at odds with the setting — that is, overcoming constraints in order to work in a certain way in spite of the setting not being set up right for that activity. An example would be neatly decorated walls that always get covered with awkwardly tacked-up easel pages, when tackboards on the walls would serve the owner much better.

---

[1]See Steele, *The Sense of Place*, ch. 5.

Group Territory

If a group within an organization has a particular territory that is more or less "owned" by them, then it can be used to sharpen the image that group projects to the rest of the organization. Almost any feature of the setting can contain messages about who the members are and what the group is doing. Graphics or pictures that depict the group's function, mission, and tasks are one of the most straightforward ways to make such a statement. If the group produces products, examples of them or working drawings and models give a sense of what is being accomplished there. Entrances to the group's area may be open or less guarded and restricted in terms of who can enter. This speaks to the separateness or exclusiveness of the group, or at least what they would like it to be.

The arrangements of workplaces, open spaces, walkways, and shared facilities (copiers, Telex machine, coffee areas, and so on) communicate about the group's modes of working and interacting. The decorations, furnishings, and colors will reflect a style of some sort, even if that style is to have no consistent style or pattern. Similarly, the group's area may have many traces of individual influence, or there may be mainly a coordinated group-as-a-whole feel to it. These each express a group identity: in the first case a tolerance for individuality; in the latter a tendency toward an overall theme (and possibly high conformity as well). Making such inferences has the same limitation as for individual workplaces, since the same setting has a different meaning depending on how it got that way — by the decision of one or a few top managers who are expressing what they want the group's image to be, or by the decisions of the membership of the group, reflecting the interests and aspirations of the users themselves.

The effects of a group's setting on the sense of identity of members depend on how expressive that setting is. If it is rich in terms of information, it may help build a sense of team cohesion, belonging, and identification with the group as a whole. If it has little visible information about the group, members may hardly be aware that they are part of a group at all, and it will not be their primary work identity. A group's setting also communicates the group's identity to other organizational groups, as well as to outside visitors. It can project the group as a force to be reckoned with (or as a relative nonentity, if the setting is bland and anonymous), as well as set expectations in others' minds about what the group can and cannot do for them. Visitors to a group area that effectively projects messages tend to be more aware of whom they are visiting and what the advantages of such a visit could be. They also tend to feel that they are in a meaningful place, somewhere with an identity. Meetings held there can be clearer, more dynamic events. They also tend to draw people back again as they seek out good place experiences.

Organizational Images

The organization's physical structures play a major role in establishing organizational images. Where facilities are located (e.g., city versus countryside) communicates how leaders see the style and mission of the organization. The design and layout of facilities communicate about the kind of work done there and the styles of working that are valued by spatial decision makers within the system. The design of access points such as entrance lobbies suggests the degree to which a system is open or closed to outsiders, while the ease of movement within the organization's facilities implies whether it is an open or closed environment for insiders themselves. The pattern of personal influences (or lack of them) by members provides a feel for how free or conforming the organization's climate tends to be.

The design and decorative themes reflect whether leaders see their system as representing the maintenance of traditional values or the experimentation with new modes of working and relating to one another.

Once again, however, the translation of these observations into inferences about the organization is a tricky one. The "look" of a system may be rigged to be what its top leaders think it *should* look like, rather than reflecting what it actually is. These are not mutually exclusive, of course. The most successful organizational settings from the point of view of a clear overall identity tend to be created when the leaders are self-analytical at the start of a design process and identify an overall concept or theme that describes the flavor of who they are and what they are in the process of becoming as an organization. Leaders who do not do this, but rather try to jump right to some design solution for how the new place should look, tend to create a surface image that is incongruent with the many more subtle indicators of organizational identity that have not received special attention (and which therefore are a cumulative record of what the system is really like). An observer should consider the prominent design choices as a statement made by the leadership, and only as that, until compared with the nitty-gritty feel of the system at many levels. There is even a particular image or feel to those organizations that have a "split personality"—a slick, controlled, well-defined corporate image expressed in a headquarters building, and many conflicting subsettings and modes of working that tend to contrast with each other when one investigates the day-to-day work settings.

The Impact of No-Person's Lands

Another possibility in organizational images is the class of settings we might call "no-person's lands"—anonymous, dull, bland areas that are ambiguous in terms of ownership and who is responsible for design or alteration, such as halls, corridors, lobby spaces, common areas near copying equipment, some conference rooms, and so on. The norms about influencing or changing such settings tend to be unclear or nonexistent, so no one feels they have the right or the responsibility for making them be alive, interesting settings. These areas therefore are left bland and personality-less, more like connectors or fillers between the "real" places such as people's offices. They have to be there for the structure, but they get treated as if they did not matter.

Unfortunately, they do matter, and they often get heavy use, such as a corridor that is a main traffic route. People's sensory experiences in such places tend to be dull and uninteresting, which in turn encourages them to tune out and pass through unconsciously. When you add up the cumulative costs of this deadening effect, the loss in human awareness and energy can be very high. This situation also sets a tone for how to survive in the organization, which is to spend a lot of time unaware of the surroundings, followed by occasional moments of focusing when tasks demand it. The danger, of course, is that people may miss the cues when important situations should be attended to right away.

The no-person's-lands environment does not "cause" such a mode of operating by itself, but it tends to encourage and reinforce it. Alternative designs can do the opposite: encourage attentiveness to and awareness of one's surroundings (both physical and social). This alternative approach starts with the assumption that no-person's lands are unhealthy, and members should take responsibility for all the areas in their setting. This mode of thinking opens up many ways to liven up dead zones: using corridors as display spaces for groups' products, graphics, ideas; holding special events in transitional areas, which helps give these areas a stronger identity as "real" places; assigning a group of people (often best if a mix of different work groups) the responsibility (and the right) of decorating and changing conference rooms to provide some variety; and taking special decorative care with the dead spots (such as external stairwells) that are used constantly but have typically received no design attention at all.

The biggest step toward doing any of these things, and therefore toward reducing the amount of dead-place experience in the system, is to make it legitimate to influence no-person's zones. The unwritten norm (nobody owns the areas exclusively, so no one should influence them) needs to change to a more conscious, explicit stance: since these areas are used by all of us, we all own them and therefore all have a joint responsibility to make them worthwhile settings.

A SENSE OF OWNERSHIP

The final point that I would like to consider in this chapter is that the nature of the workplace affects people's sense of ownership and involvement in their organization and group. A strong sense of identity, encouraged by the ways described here, tends to lead people to both a sense of individuality (I know more about who I am) and a sense of community (I know what I am a part of and I feel that I share joint ownership and responsibility for it). Many organizational leaders appear to believe the opposite, that allowing people to express their individual preferences in their workplace design will destroy a sense of community. But I think that if it is done well (such as through the processes described in Part II), the cumulative effect on people who are able to participate in spatial decisions is that they have a stronger sense of ownership in the community of the organization, not a weaker one. Their combined influences on the workplace can generate a stronger sense of identity (because it is an accurate reflection or record of users' real desires and modes of working) than can a single integrated design imposed on everyone by a mandate from the top leaders.

A Dutch insurance company called Central Beheer engaged in a design process that represents a positive example of promoting in their employees a sense of personal ownership of a new facility.[2] The decision to build a new headquarters was based in part on a serious personnel turnover problem. They decided to move the headquarters out of Amsterdam and hired internationally known Dutch architect Herman Hertzberger to create an environment that would truly feel like "home" to the users and thus be likely to increase the employees' sense of identification with and loyalty to the company. Hertzberger's orientation could be described (in a great oversimplification) as "architecture for users, not for architects." He created a striking, complex structure with rough finishes and many different kinds of spaces — large areas, small nooks, balconies, and the like. But the key was the notion that the building was the *beginning* of the design and creation process, not the end of it. It was made to encourage and require the touches of its users in order to be functional, and

[2]See Francis Duffy, "Appraisal," *The Architects' Journal* (London) 29 (October 1975): 893–904.

both the designer and the company encouraged users to make it their own by personalizing both individual workplaces and common areas. Plants, graphics, banners, personal furniture, and the like were all considered to be a natural part of bringing the building to life as a real place — not just something to be tolerated if a few people wanted to be stubborn, as is often the attitude of top management when they commission a new building.

The results seem to support the original goals quite well. People have indeed made the building their own, in ways both predictable and unpredictable. They also feel great pride in it and bring family and friends to visit more often than to the old building, treating the new one somewhat like an extension of their homes. Turnover has also gone down dramatically, probably because of both the stronger sense of identification with place as well as the new location in a much smaller city than Amsterdam.

An opposite example is represented by a headquarters building in this country that I have visited a number of times. It has twenty floors of offices on long, double-loaded corridors with a big elevator core in the center. There is very little visible information anywhere in the building about what the company does, which groups occupy which areas, and who the individual occupants are. There are essentially no graphics or decorations in any halls, except on the top executive floor (where there are specially chosen artworks), and no names on any doors, only numbers.

The effect on a visitor is somewhat eerie. In spite of the considerable time I have spent there, I still feel as if it is one large no-person's land. The effects on those who work there are more subtle but also probably more severe. Occupants seem to be hardened to working in an anonymous, expressionless environment, and in fact to feel that this is the way it has to be in a business corporation. Of course there are exceptions among the members — people who have started to experiment with more expressive use of their workplaces — but they talk about this as representing a personal risk of violating unwritten corporate standards that encourage anonymity and uniformity.

The point here is not that every person in the first example ought to go wild with interior decoration activities in the new building, nor that all employees in the second building ought to feel anger at being constrained in their personal expression. It is simply that a structure and setting that encourage those who choose to express themselves in the ways they influence and use their workplaces will be more likely to incline people toward a personal sense of ownership of that setting, no matter what its faults. In the Central Beheer headquarters, employees express real fondness for the place; in the second case, employees say that the headquarters is important to the history of the company and probably is not so awful, really. . . . They are resigned to low expectations for what a working environment can be.

Top executives often seem to take actions that effectively encourage a low level of aspiration as far as sense of identity with one's workplace is concerned. My experiences suggest that this is mainly because they fear "chaos" if they were to reduce control over the work setting and allow or actually encourage greater individuality of environmental influence. They fear that it would not reflect a clear identity for the organization as a whole. And yet, the sum of the groups and individuals that make up the system *is* its identity, or at least a major one. If they trusted such a notion, they could follow the Central Beheer example and create a strong basic setting with rich potential for individualization, and thereby end up with a setting that expressed both individuality and the sense of identity of the whole.

SUMMARY

The sense of identity is an important aspect of being centered and using energy well, for individuals, groups, and an organization as a whole. Workplaces can enhance or degrade that sense of identity, both by how they look and the processes that are used to design them. No-person's lands do the opposite — they tend to make employees feel transient and likely to block out their immediate surroundings. Finally, settings that promote personalization tend to generate a sense of owner ship in the users, which means they identify more with both the place and the organization.

CHAPTER 9

Social Interaction

Probably the most far-reaching effect of the office-type work environment structure is that it tends to shape the nature of interactions among employees, as well as between them and outsiders. It affects both the quantity and quality of contacts and is one of the visible types of environmental influence that most office workers are aware of to some degree. What we tend to be unaware of, however, is the extent of such influence: the way probabilities of contact are influenced and specific events are shaped. This is also an important effect for our purposes because so much of organizational life is interaction of one sort or another: people trying to influence or communicate with each other and thereby make things happen. As mentioned earlier, the physical setting affects the amount of energy or effort that a given interpersonal contact will require, which in turn affects the probability that someone will choose to do it or not, based on whether they feel the result will be worth the cost.

MODES OF SOCIAL CONTACT IN AN ORGANIZATION

Work Information Sharing.   This refers to those interactions at work primarily involved in getting a job done, such as going to someone's workplace to convey or ask for information, holding a meeting to share information or work on a problem together, telling someone that you have arrived at the office and are available for contact when she is ready, making a telephone call to share or seek information, and so on. Generally speaking, these kinds of interactions will occur in almost any environment if people feel they are essential to fulfilling their roles in the organization. The issue for these interactions from a work setting viewpoint is, at what cost do they occur? How easy or difficult is it to do them, and to what extent will someone tend to put off contacts or just drop an idea as not worth the effort? A related issue is the quality of the interaction. For example, when a meeting is held, does the setting allow the participants to really focus and understand each other, or does it contain distractions that tend to muddy the communications process?

Casual Contacts.   These day-to-day interactions that occur more by chance than by plan are not seen as essential to performing the work role well. Nodding to people whose desks you pass each morning on the way to your own is such an interaction, as is regularly chatting with someone near the coffee machine or in the copying room. Going to lunch with those people who are near your own workplace (or those who are not, for that matter) fits this type, as does professionals standing in a hallway sharing state-of-the-art ideas about new technical developments. In the aggregate these contacts represent a fairly large percentage of the interactions in most work groups, but they tend to be unplanned and somewhat invisible to the people themselves.

Social Observation and Control.   These interactions are not really a separate class so much as another function that social contacts serve for members of an organization. As explained in Chapter 4, every social system needs some predictability about how members will behave, what tasks they will perform, and in what style. The primary means of assessing compliance with rules, policies, and norms is through social interaction, that is, people observing one another so as to judge whether they are behaving in acceptable ways or not. Thus both work-oriented and casual contacts provide opportunities for such observations.

Special Events.   From time to time in every organization special events happen: large-scale convocations, parties, gatherings of members to learn about or respond to a crisis situation, diagnostic events planned to help members become more aware of how well they are working with each other, awards ceremonies, and so on. This type of event may be planned or spontaneous, work-focused or social, but it represents enough of a departure from "business as usual" to feel different and to have a special impact on people who are a part of the event (as well as on people who were not).

These four types of social interaction are not meant to be mutually exclusive categories. They simply provide a means for being relatively concrete when talking about the ecological impact of settings on the interaction processes in an organization.[1] In the rest of this chapter I will il-

---

[1] For a comprehensive treatment of the effects of physical environment on social contact, see Robert Sommer, *Personal Space: The Behavioral Basis of Design* (Englewood Cliffs, N.J.,: Prentice-Hall, 1969), or E. T. Hall, *The Hidden Dimension* (Garden City, N.Y.: Doubleday, 1966).

lustrate ways of perceiving such influences on each of the four types of
contact in organizations so that we can make these influences be what
we would like.

INFLUENCES OF THE SETTING

On Work Contacts

One of the simplest influences on work interactions comes from
physical distances: how far is it from one person's workplace to another?
This distance affects the perceived (and real) effort that it takes to get
to see someone face-to-face. There are really two factors here: actual
distance and "functional" distance, that is, the amount of difficulty involved in getting from point A to point B. Being on adjacent floors of a
building, separated by only ten feet and a ceiling/floor, can require a long
walk and an elevator ride in order to go from one office to another. It
is a short actual distance but long functional one. Locations of walls, door-
ways, stairways, walkways, and banks of elevators all play a part in determining how much effort it takes for people to have face-to-face contact
with each other, and therefore how frequently they will do it.

I have seen several instances where an apparently simple physical
change, done for purposes of cost savings or consolidation of space, had
an unanticipated effect on communication. For example, when one organizational group moves out of the main building into another one
because they need more space, the impact is on contacts with members
of groups left behind. The greater the separation the bigger the impact,
even though that was not the original intent of the move and everyone
assured themselves that they would continue to meet in the same ways
they always had because it was vital to getting the job done. It just does
not happen, as people find reasons to put off going from one building to
the other or save up issues to talk about until they have a "package" of
things to do in the other building. Timeliness of discussions is minimized,
and opportunities for mutual influence before actions are taken tend to
decrease, not because people want it, but because it is the net effect of
its being harder to get together as often.

Simple proximities within a given group's area — whose workplaces
are adjacent and whose are separated — can affect the day-to-day sharing of work information, although they will not control it altogether, since
people will usually still make the essential contacts even if they take some
effort. Relations between the head of a group and other members are
probably the most heavily affected by proximity, so that the location of
the head person's workplace becomes a significant layout decision. De-

pending on what you want to encourage in the way of contacts between boss and subordinates, you can locate them so as to increase or decrease the natural frequency of such contacts.

At the simplest level, there are very basic effects of layout on information sharing. If two people need to be sharing fast-changing information all day long, putting them adjacent and visible to one another is almost mandatory (although it may not be done in groups where having a separate, private office is considered a reflection of importance or status).

Another key effect of settings on contacts is the extent of regular *interference* with the communication process that is caused by the physical setting. Interference is often caused by noise factors, as with one factory management team I observed who held regular meetings of eight to ten people in a conference area set up on a shop floor. This area was under a giant air blower and duct system, so that it was almost impossible to hear someone who was sitting more than five feet away in the meeting. The net results were meetings where many points were not understood, people did other personal work and did not take part, and adjacent members held many side conversations. Those meetings had people who were physically present but psychologically absent.

Interferences can also be human, as when two people who are trying to talk quietly are always interrupted by people using their workplace as a pass-through trafficway to another area. The more private the conversation is supposed to be, the more impossible such a structure will be in terms of real communication. A third type of interference is a poor communications technology, such as a telephone system that is unreliable or slow to make connections. The cumulative cost of such a system is enormous, and it is more economical to get such communication networks designed right for your needs.[2]

On Casual Contacts

Some of the same physical features just described will obviously impact informal interactions the same way they do necessary work contacts, and in fact in a stronger manner. People who are separated by large distances or barriers are clearly less likely to strike up conversations than are those who are near to each other every day. Relative locations of offices help shape friendship patterns and the flow of grapevine informa-

---

[2]For a more detailed discussion of the use of settings for social contacts, see chapter 5 of F. Steele, *Physical Settings and Organization Development* (Reading, Mass.: Addison-Wesley, 1973).

tion, just by who is available to tell or be asked about current events. Visibility plays a big part in casual contact because people who are able to see each other (at work, or coming and going) tend to be more aware of each other. "Out of sight, out of mind" has a lot of validity when it comes to being aware of people whom we are not required by the nature of our jobs to take into account.

In this regard, the presence or absence of communal areas in the organization is a big influence on the pattern of informal contacts and communication. I once consulted to an organization that was housed in a former apartment building that had been adapted to be a corporate headquarters. There were no central gathering spaces and it was possible (and even likely) that someone would come to work in the morning, go up on the elevator to her floor, into her office, spend the day, and go home without ever having seen another member of the organization (certainly none outside her immediate group, although there were not even group spaces per se). It was very hard in that organization to get a real feel for the climate or mood at any particular time, nor were people particularly aware of being a part of the corporate headquarters.

The members' general sense of connection and identification with the whole was quite low until the organization created a new headquarters building designed to have the opposite characteristics. In the new building a modified open plan was used with personal workplaces and visible areas so that the activities of the system were observable. It was possible to tell that there were other people in the building, which was not the case in the old one. In the new building there were many *magnet facilities*: common facilities located and structured so as to draw people together and encourage informal contact. These were a well-designed cafeteria, coffee areas on different floors, copying facilities and other shared equipment, and seating areas that were not just thrown into leftover spots but thoughtfully located where they could be used without interference or discomfort. These features represent ways of increasing the probability that members will have informal contacts day-to-day, thus being more aware of each other, of what is going on in the system, and of how they personally fit into the organization.

Another example of a building designed to promote desired informal contacts is the Decker Engineering Building designed by Davis, Brody for Corning Glass Works. The layout is based on Thomas Allen's research on the work patterns of researchers and scientists:

> Dr. Allen's findings showed that more than 80 percent of an engineer's ideas come from face-to-face contact with colleagues. They dislike using the phone, will not walk more than 100 feet to discuss

an idea or gather information, and avoid using elevators. "Distance," Dr. Allen says, "delays interaction."

Davis, Brody deftly translated Dr. Allen's findings into a three-story structure that has optimum visibility of every floor, strategically placed ramps, stairs and escalators to encourage vertical movement, and an open plan layout and informal gathering places for maximum communication — all within a fully flexible framework.[3]

Seating arrangement is another physical feature that tends to very concretely affect social interaction. There is a fairly large body of research concerning the impact of seating patterns on communication, such as in meetings where people who can *see* each other (seated across a table from one another) are more likely to interact than are those who are not visible (lined up in a row along one side of a rectangular table). This is why round or oval tables are recommended if you are trying to promote a truly interactive group discussion, versus just wanting to have a group of people be an *audience* for what you want to tell them.[4]

Finally, if you want to create a setting that encourages informal contact, it is recommended that you not try to make it so "cost efficient" that layouts are very tight and almost every square foot is identified as either someone's workplace or a circulation corridor. When people are having chance, casual contacts, they will be uncomfortable and cut them short if they are always in the way in someone's territory. There need to be some areas or free zones that belong to everybody, so that unplanned contacts can take place there.

On Social Control

One of the often overlooked functions of settings in an organization is the provision of means for social control: the application and enforcement of policies and social norms on the members of the system, so that there is some predictability or pattern to what people will and will not do there. Different features of the physical setting have different effects on this process of social control, some aiding and some blocking it.[5]

[3]See "Corning Glass Design Spurs Engineers' Creativity," *Facilities Management* (January 1982): 43–49.

[4]Sommer has researched the impact of seating arrangements on pulling people together ("sociopetal space") or pushing them apart ("socio-fugal space"). See Sommer, *Personal Space*.

[5]For interesting studies on the impact of design on social control processes, see Oscar Newman, *Defensible Space* (New York: Macmillan, 1973).

(Which is better depends on whether you think there should be more conformity to norms or more freedom for individualistic actions.)

Some features tend to enhance people's ability to enforce norms on one another in a group or organization. Standardized equipment and furniture, plus standardized sizes of workspaces, generally push people toward similar arrangements and uses of their workspaces. Some groups have norms about the "right" ways to set up one's office, and such standardization makes big variations in layout unlikely. The same is true for fragile, soft wall surfaces on which it is hard to hang decorations. If there are norms against personalization (because the place would lose its "integrated design" look), then unsuitable wall surfaces tend to discourage such tinkering. Locations or layouts where people are scattered or separated, so that no one is regularly sitting near anyone else in a workspace, tend to reduce the probability of influence attempts, just because interactions tend to be fewer. Similarly, if the physical structure is such that everyone's workplace is closed off and hidden from view, then there is more scope for people to do whatever they want in their own offices. I once saw a company where management had installed clear glass windows in office doors, ostensibly for light, but also presumably for surveillance purposes. Occupants promptly covered the windows with posters or banners, which elicited a formal policy statement that henceforth people were to leave their windows uncovered. This confirmed people's view that top management suspected that all sorts of deviant behaviors were happening behind those closed doors. People paid no attention to the policy and left the windows covered (and management to brood). The most extreme layout in terms of surveillance of possible deviant behavior is the bull-pen arrangement, where everyone sits together in an open room. In such an arrangement, a supervisor often sits in a cubicle at the back where he or she can see everyone but not necessarily be seen by others.

Features that discourage easy enforcement of norms tend in part to be the mirror images of high-control features. As mentioned, private spaces with no overlooking access are one example. Scattered layouts where there are no central activity spaces tend to make group influence harder than layouts where a large number of people spend time in the same area with one another. If the materials in a workplace — walls, furniture, floor, lighting, and so on — are durable and allow easy adjustments and tinkering, then people will be more likely to use their workplaces in varied, nonstandard ways. Relative locations of whole groups play a part in the degree to which organizational norms are enforced on a group and its members. Groups that are located in visible, high-traffic areas where many people can observe them generally feel that they have to "play the game" and abide by various norms relating to workplace layout, dress codes, work times, and the like. This is why managers who are trying to start a new group with the explicit goal of being innovative about work methods or products will often try to find a location that is secluded, where they can develop unobserved for a period of time. This allows them to test new methods and demonstrate their usefulness whereas if they were in a more central, visible location they would be subject to pressures to stop deviating and conform to accepted practices. They could not produce tangible results without a good deal of energy being wasted in justifying their departures from the norms. It is usually more efficient to structure the physical setting so that they have the freedom initially to go their own way unobserved.

On Special Events

One kind of setting I have come to view as a potent but generally underappreciated influence on the nature of social interactions in an organization is the *forum for special events*. When I use this phrase I envision a relatively central space (accessible to many different groups in the organization) that is flexibly structured (seating arrangements can be easily set up or changed, seats can be removed altogether, the space can be divided into smaller spaces) and is sufficiently large to contain at one time a fair percentage of the occupants of that location (i.e., the people who work for the organization in that building). Many organizations have no such forum, and the closest thing to it is a moderately sized conference room in some out-of-the-way spot or a meeting room in a hotel.

It is hard to measure the effect of this lack on social interaction since it is a negative effect of what *does not* happen. Members generally are not aware of what is missing. The best way to see the difference is to observe those organizations that do have such a forum. These organizations tend to communicate more through discussions and presentations to large groups, to experiment or innovate with crossgroup combination meetings to deal with intergroup issues, to hold more spontaneous events (since they do not require the reserving of an outside facility), and to have unplanned events that occur when people happen to gather in the forum space. My consulting experiences have convinced me that systems that lack such a space tend to put off or not hold such events at all and they are less able to quickly influence the dynamics and directions of internal events when such gatherings do not occur. The obvious analogy here is to the agorae or forums in ancient Greek and Roman cities. They were centers of the community's influence process, and an organization can be thought of as a community that requires a similar give-and-take in order to be a dynamic institution.

SETTINGS, INTERACTION, AND PRIVACY

The final issue I would like to address in this chapter is the tension that exists between the need for stimulation (from contacts with other people) and the need for privacy (being able to withdraw from contacts and be on one's own). Both are human needs, with neither being inherently better than the other. It is therefore a diagnostic question whether an individual's personal style and job role call for him to be in contact with others or to be in a relatively withdrawn spot not available to others. High-quality settings, from this standpoint, are those that allow people to control contacts and to have a choice about when and how much interaction they have with others.

In the past, it was assumed that the more private a workspace was, the better it was. Privacy was one of the symbols in the physical language of social status in an organization. Entry-level employees were in the open; as you moved a little higher up, you shared an office with one or two others; finally at some level (varying from organization to organization) you arrived at a "private" office with walls and a door. At the very top, you had not only a private office but also an outer office with minions to screen unwanted contacts for you. The advent of an era of scarce resources, diminishing stability of layouts, and greater thoughtfulness about organizational design has led to a more complex picture in this area. The open-plan and modified open-plan layouts have led to the necessity for people to live without traditional private offices, although "modified open plan" all too often means that people's workplaces are in an interior landscape configuration *except* if they are above a certain hierarchical level, where once again the office with walls and a door is the reward for having climbed the ladder of success. This approach, with tightened space but unchanged assumptions (about privacy = good = high status), tends to generate a good deal of resentment and stress in members who feel their needs are being sacrificed so that the organization can cut total square footage and alterations costs.

I believe that many of these stresses are a direct result of poor or partial planning. Layouts should be done using line-of-sight guidelines, rather than having people staring directly at one another when at their normal working spots. This leads to a felt lack of visual privacy, which is common but not inherent in open-plan layouts. As for audial privacy, there are many open layouts that are too dense, contain too many hard, reflective surfaces, or have too low a level of ambient sound so that conversations are not masked. The same is true in many "closed" plans, where paper-thin walls or heating and ventilation ducts transmit conversations to adjacent offices. Closed offices provide visual separation, but they are no guarantee of audial privacy. In fact, they may provide a false sense of security when people should instead be aware that they can be easily overheard.

Since interaction and withdrawal are both reasonable needs for members of an organization, the layout that makes the most sense to me, in principle, is one that allows people *choice* over whether to be interacting or withdrawn, public or private. (It is the feeling of lack of control over one's contacts that is the basis for the stress described above.) A single workplace does not necessarily have to meet both these criteria; in many cases it cannot.

One alternative model that I think has great promise is a kind of "cave and court" design, where members have very small, private withdrawal spots (the caves) that are meant only for that purpose, and not as symbols of importance or as places to which subordinates must flock at the occupants' convenience. Then for meeting, talking, being available to visitors, watching what others are doing, and so on, there are a variety of more public workplaces (the courts), laid out as conference rooms, sitting rooms, and open-plan common areas. Very confidential conversations and telephone calls can occur in the caves, as can high-concentration tasks; stimulative, contact-oriented activities can occur better in the court areas than in layouts that are essentially just an aggregate of workplaces, which are a little of each and not very good for either function.

The combined influence of physical structure and social norms on people's sense of self-control over stimulation and withdrawal activities is another important factor. Many closed, cellular layouts are especially costly to members' effectiveness because the system lacks social norms that encourage people to change scenes for different activities, to get out of their separate workplaces and circulate in order to stay in touch with the realities of the system (versus maintaining the dated views they have if they remain sequestered in their offices). Conversely, many open-plan layouts feel unacceptable or unlivable because occupants have not worked out new norms for controlling interruptions and intrusions (which were handled by visible physical barriers in the old cellular plan). In either type of plan the needs of the organization will require more interaction at some times, more separation at others. Neither physical layout is likely to facilitate such varying modes of operating unless the physical *and* social systems are thought of and designed as an organic, reciprocal whole.

SUMMARY

This chapter has provided some illustrations of the ways in which workplace layout and design affect the quantity and quality of social interaction in an organization. The physical setting tends to influence interaction in four broad areas: work task contacts, casual contacts, contacts that provide social control, and special events that cut across organizational boundaries. In each case the setting can promote or discourage such contacts, and it is a diagnostic question as to how much and what kinds of contacts should be encouraged. The last point considered was organizational members' needs for both social interaction and privacy. Some suggestions were made about how to provide people with some choice and control over the pattern of contacts with other people at work. The cave-and-court design was suggested as an effective design for upper management levels.

CHAPTER 10

Settings and Vitality:
Generating Energy and Intensity

The third dimension affecting the impact of settings on organizational life is harder to observe than social interactions. It is the extent to which there is a sense of high energy and excitement in the organization — whether there is a sense of *intensity*, of aliveness to the organization as an entity in its environment. This chapter will explore some of the ways in which organizational energy and intensity are influenced by a system's physical settings, keeping in mind that these settings are not the only contributors to organizational vitality. The style of management, the types of people recruited, the opportunities in markets or tasks, and the general social environment in which the organization operates are other factors that are beyond the focus of this chapter.

THE CONCEPTS OF ORGANIZATIONAL ENERGY AND EXCITEMENT

The concept of organizational energy as a variable within systems is a relatively recent development, probably being best explained by Barry Oshry, a Boston-based behavioral scientist who has done pioneering work in the dynamics of social systems.[1] In Oshry's terms, organizational energy is the potential for action by members of the organization, either individually or collectively. The energy is focused if there is a tendency for members to act toward the same ends, and it is diffuse or unfocused if the members use their energy to act independently.

---

[1]Oshry has written a series of papers that develop this view of organizations as organisms. See, for example, "Organic Power," "Power and Position," and "Middle Power," all of which are available from P.S.T., Inc., P.O. Box 388, Prudential Station, Boston, Mass. 02199.

The energy in a human system obviously comes from the members. It is their willingness to *do* something that creates the potential for action. This willingness in turn stems from people caring enough about something to act on it. This can mean positive motivation of wanting something: to achieve personal or organizational goals; to meet a challenge; to make a lot of money; to be recognized by superiors, peers, or subordinates as having made a contribution; to learn new skills by trying new things; or to take risks as a way of generating internal excitement. Anything that someone wants is a potential energizer, and people who can cause others to see a connection between acting and getting what they want will be able to focus the system's energy in certain directions.

There is also great energy potential in the class of emotions that some people would call "negative" — anger, frustration, resentment, tension, anxiety, fear, and so on. These can be energizers if people take to action, if people see a connection between their actions and being able to resolve these feelings in some satisfying manner.

Without going into too much detail here, we can assume that one way in which individuals' energies for action will add up to directed systemic energy is when their actions are aimed in the same direction — that is, when they see themselves as having a shared identity and caring about the same things. The opposite situation can also be a strong system energizer: sharpening differentiations within a system clarifies for people who shares their interests and concerns. As in the case of union organizers, this raises people's awareness that they may be more likely to have an effect (about getting what they want, making things happen, or reducing conditions that anger them) if they act together as a subgroup. Ironically, sharpening differences (so that subgroups can see who have common interests and who do not) can be a healthy move to induce members to act and resolve systemic issues that have frustrated everyone because of lack of productive action. This goes against the more conventional wisdom of many managers who believe that "polarizing" a situation will always lead to a stalemate and is therefore a bad thing to do. My experience says that the inaction is usually caused because issues are *already* polarized in an unclear, nondiscussable manner; getting the positions out in the open tends to release energy to resolve the issues.

A related variable that can also be affected by the physical setting is organizational intensity, a major aspect of the climate of an organization. Members sense it as "something in the air" that affects how they in turn feel when they come to work. It has a number of components. One is a sense of common mission or direction: a shared image of where the organization is headed, why it is worth getting there, and how individual and group actions contribute to achieving this overall mission. Another is a sense of common identity (as discussed in Chapter 8), that members share some fundamental values and interests. Conversely, the sense of differentiation, of where the tensions are between subgroups, can feel like a challenge and therefore be a source of intensity — *if* the members also feel that there is a commitment to the organization's overall mission. Members in a climate of organizational intensity can visualize exciting possibilities for the future and believe that they really are possible, not just pipe dreams being generated by leaders who wish that members would feel excited and willing to put their energy wholeheartedly into the organization's tasks. True organizational intensity is reflected in excitement among the members.[2]

PHYSICAL INFLUENCES ON ENERGY AND EXCITEMENT

Focused human energy and a climate of organizational intensity are important variables in the operation of an organization. Managers should think of themselves as managing energy and excitement, among other things, and should strive to understand how these factors can be influenced in desired directions. The rest of this chapter will discuss some of the main ways in which physical settings have an impact on intensity and the use of organizational energy and excitement in a human system. This is not meant to be the definitive theory of system energy, nor a how-to-do-it set of rules for designing workspaces that are energizing and exciting. It should stimulate readers to be aware of the ways in which seemingly simple choices (such as where to locate offices within a group's spaces) often have rather strong effects on the amount and use of energy within that group, effects that may or may not be what you would like to have happen.

Relative Locations

Location is probably the most all-encompassing and potent physical variable: the configuration of people in relation to other group members and the locations of groups in relation to other groups and activity centers in the organization. For example, people who work near each other all day are more likely to be aware of common interests, concerns, needs, and frustrations than those who are scattered and see each other only oc-

---

[2]I am grateful to Oron South and David Berlew for their stimulating and interesting ideas concerning the concepts of organizational intensity and excitement.

casionally. A manager who wants to enhance such awareness of com-
monalities and to influence the directions of resulting actions will tend
to group workplaces together; one who does not want this awareness to
develop and fears its consequences will tend to scatter people and make
it hard for them to come together.

The location of power people also has an effect on system energy.
People tend to be more on edge or alert when the boss is around and visible every day than when he or she is hidden away in some private "inner
sanctum." In this sense, I believe the impact of the workers' being visible to the boss is overrated (although some of the tension comes from people's feelings that they are being evaluated moment-to-moment) and the
effect of the boss being visible to the workers is underrated (since it is this
visibility that stimulates people to feel concerned about their performance
for a powerful audience).[3]

Locations play a straightforward role in the use of energy by determining how easy or difficult it is for people to interact with one another.
If two groups occupy separate buildings yet must interact regularly to
fulfill their basic tasks, then considerable energy is used in traveling between the two locations or in deciding whether and when to bother to
make a trip to the other group's location. Conversely, a separation between two groups can be a positive energizer by developing each group's
sense of identity and mission. But this has to be tested against the energy
costs of the separation, with a balance being drawn between the two.
It is possible to structure a group's workplace to create a clear sense of
identity and purpose, yet have it be inefficient because every action requires a great deal of physical or psychological effort. As noted in Chapter
9, this effect can also be caused not by sheer distance separation but by
"obstacle separation" where it is problematic to go from point A to point
B (no passages through, having to take an unreliable elevator, having to
go through another group's spaces, and so on). The effect is the same in
that it wastes energy and discourages face-to-face interaction.

Visibility

One way of differentiating organizational workplace designs is the
extent to which *visibility* is a feature, so that people can see one another
and see what is happening in the system day-to-day. Besides location

---

[3]A similar effect may be created by the management style called "management by
wandering around," where the boss is very mobile, seeing what is happening and being
seen. This helps people feel that they are actively involved. See Thomas J. Peters and Charles
Waterman, Jr., *In Search of Excellence* (New York: Harper & Row, 1982).

(described above), there are other factors that impact on visibility: the type of structure — open-plan versus closed offices; whether there is a linear spread of workplaces or if they are concentrated around a central core; the availability of centrally located meeting spaces where people can see who is with whom at a given time versus having such spots hidden on the edges of the system; and the nature of materials used in workplaces — glass walls versus dry wall, and so on. All these factors impact on how much members will be able to see of the workings of the organization. I believe that observation stimulates human awareness, concerns, and interests, both consciously and unconsciously. People who see what is happening are more likely to think of their own connections with system goals, to be aware of possibilities, to know when it is time to act so as to influence events in a desired direction, to sense when they should be worried or concerned, and to find out more about what is happening so as to protect their interests.

Visibility is, in my mind, one of the more important stimulators of system energy and excitement. However, there are leaders who fear that the results of increased employee energy levels and excitement will be unpredictable, uncontrollable, and therefore negative from the point of view of their own power. From this stance they should probably structure low visibility systems that tend to downplay awareness of current events and future possibilities, and put the emphasis on control of energy.

Ambient Environment Features

The most obvious set of features that impact human energy in a work setting are those ambient features with a direct physiological impact on individuals' energy levels and abilities to engage in sustained action. These features include the type and intensity of light; desks, chairs, and other furniture, and whether they were specifically chosen to allow an individual to maintain good balance and positioning for their bodies; ambient temperature levels and whether they match individuals' physical activity levels (e.g., not too cold or hot while sitting, not too hot while moving around); and amount and kinds of sound and how well they can be controlled as people engage in different tasks. Any of these features can be a major energy drain if not appropriate to the users' needs. Poor lighting levels result in eye strain; overly warm rooms lead to lethargy and drowsiness; overly noisy settings require extra energy to be expended simply on concentrating to hear what others are saying; and badly chosen furniture can lead to recurring back and other problems that sap people of their vitality. The point is fairly obvious: vitality requires that these physiologically related features of settings be in balance and matched to the users or there will be a cumulative drain on the energy level of both individuals and the system as a whole. The hidden point worth considering is that this cumulative effect can be much larger and more costly than suspected. If this view were kept in mind, there would be less tolerating of unsatisfactory features of settings and a lot more attempting to make them what they should be for stimulating vitality.

Size and Density of Spaces

The tradeoff of size and density of spaces versus costs per square foot tends to generate much conflict in workplace design. The figure of square footage per person is sometimes used as a measure of the efficient use of a facility, with the assumption being that the smaller the total space needed for a given number of people, the more efficiently an installation is being used. When we think in terms of task accomplishment, and particularly impact on energy level and use of energy by occupants, the question of efficiency becomes much more complicated than minimizing square feet per person. For example, office areas that are too dense, with people interfering with each other's freedom of movement, tend to sap a lot of human energy through people just coping with the stresses of this crowding. Assuming that the organization's reason for existence is to do something, not simply to house people in as small an area as possible, this is not necessarily an *efficient* use of space, it is just a *minimal* use of space.

In the opposite direction, I have seen work areas that were too large for the numbers of people using them. As I described before, the shrinking organization that remains in unaltered work settings experiences an energy drain, owing not to interference but to what might be called "nostalgic depression." The setting depresses users by being a constant reminder of better times and of the fact that the trend for the organization is not growth but decline. Even when occupants justify staying in their old configuration because it is theoretically a good deal for everyone to have more space, I think the pessimistic mood it creates costs more to the group in total than the extra room is worth to the individuals.

Decoration and Color

This is an area where there have been numerous attempts to apply the research findings of environmental psychology in a direct, cause-and-effect manner. (Something that is generally hard to do in workplace design.) Fairly consistent findings indicate that a particular range of colors — red, yellow, orange — tends to be excitatory or stimulating, while "cooler" colors — blues, greys, and the like — tend to have a calming effect. To some degree this can be applied in workplace decoration, depending on the goals one has for how stimulating a setting should be to its users. Colors need to be used very thoughtfully, however, since there are many other factors that come into play: decorative and symbolic traditions of the user group (i.e., what is the cultural meaning of warm or cool colors for them?), the nature of the particular tasks being done in that spot, the types of natural and artificial lighting, and what kind of decorative setting the people were in before the present one. In general, I am skeptical that decorative elements such as color can be used by themselves to create an inherently stimulating and exciting setting. But the reverse is easier to do: drab colors, dull surroundings with no decorative elements, and the like, seem more certain to have a depressing effect on users' energy levels and willingness to take action. It is easier to tone a system down than it is to spark it to higher energy levels.

Graphic Representations
of Organizational Activities

One of the most interesting features of workplaces is the presence or absence of visual clues about what the group or organization is doing or planning to do in the future. Displays of actual physical products or models of products, facilities, and so forth give daily passersby a sense of what the system is doing and how they fit into it. Models or plans for future products can be displayed in central locations and provide a real sense of excitement about the system's future possibilities. Being able to see what is coming up is a much more potent stimulator of people's energy to make it happen than is being told about it in a speech or memorandum. Even pictures of products or of activities at the organization's other locations can increase occupants' awareness of the whole system and what they should be doing to maintain it. Some organizations' work is just naturally visually exciting, such as advertising agencies or architecture and planning firms; they have an inherent advantage using graphics in interesting ways. I think that any organization has the potential to use this medium to generate a sense of excitement, if the leaders are willing to take the trouble to be inventive about ways of representing the system's mission, activities, and future in graphic form.

Operational Centers: Accessibility

As mentioned earlier, visibility is a key factor in generating a sense of organizational intensity among members of a system. Another feature that can enhance the impact of visibility is *accessibility*, especially the accessibility of information about what is happening in the organization and in its environment. As I see it, this accessibility is most likely to exist if there is an operational *center* to the facility where people work. By this I mean a central location where people go to acquire information, check rumors, test ideas, and the like. This could be a central operations room, a common area with central files, or an electronic media center with access to many types of private and public information sources. Such a center allows people to test ideas, seek out patterns, and understand what is happening in the surrounding environment in a way that is not wasteful of energy through helter-skelter searching for some source that might be able to help them get what they want.

Although office workers sometimes think of central files and data sources as an attempt by the organization's leaders to eliminate personal files and records, I think that the center concept (if the operations center is set up right, so that it is truly efficient for people to use) can be useful, because the whole system *and* individuals can have a greater intensity about their work processes. Many office facilities have no such center, and information-seeking activities are dispersed and diffused throughout the organization. I doubt if the leaders in such an organization are aware of the difference between a diffuse layout and one that has an operational center. The possible effects on the level of organizational intensity can usually only be sensed by setting up such a center and experiencing the differences in how people use their time and energies.

Flexibility

One of the characteristics of workplaces that can be most useful in maintaining a high-quality use of system energy is *flexibility*, both in structures and in relative locations of individuals and groups. The spatial needs of an organization change over time, and on the average they probably change much more rapidly today than they did twenty years ago. Physical settings that have a relatively permanent structure tend to become more and more mismatched with the users they are supposed to serve and to be an increasing drag on the energy of members as they adapt their work activities to the outdated setting.

For example, if an organization makes extensive use of temporary task forces or project teams, their facilities should be flexible enough to allow creation of operational centers for the teams' activities, where information can be collected and events can be held that help to build a shared sense of the teams as functioning entities. If teams do not create a special place that is theirs for the life of the project, they will have trouble developing a strong sense of shared identity and clear images of possible group accomplishments.

In instances where the physical structures (dispersed offices, no central place, no symbolic images of who the group is and what it is about) are left unchanged, managers argue that it is cheaper to do it that way than to make temporary adjustments and relocations. My experience suggests the opposite: any time you do not make adjustments in physical structures for a project team you are likely to incur very high hidden costs. Being inflexible about arrangements can cost a great deal in low energy and decreased excitement about the team and its mission. If it is worth creating the team at all, it is worth giving the team the best arrangements for doing well.

SUMMARY

The scattered task force is one example of a physical setting pattern that tends to drain the energy of its users. Another is the closed, dispersed structure where permanent work groups are scattered out of sight of one another, so that they have no visual reminders of who else is in the system or what is going on. The "courthouse" style building with long, double-loaded corridors (office doors on each side of the corridor, which runs down the center or around the building) is such a setting. It lacks any center of activity, so that the only community areas are traffic ways. People generally interact only in pairs as they encounter each other in the halls, and there is no forum for spontaneous group events.

Settings that are devoid of graphic images relating to the organization's tasks tend to be low-excitement settings, as do ones where all decorative elements are dictated from the top. There is no sense of the cumulative efforts of members at making a setting their own. Poor physiological impact (bad lighting, too much noise, uncomfortable furniture) has been mentioned as an obvious energy-draining environment, as are settings where people are crowded too closely together to control the level of contacts they have with one another. Inflexible settings are a detriment to people's energy and excitement, as users are forced to work harder and harder to use settings that are no longer appropriate to their demands and needs.

Additional considerations of system energy and its effects will be presented in the discussion of organizational climate in Chapter 14 and in the specific applications of organizational ecology to executive teams in Chapter 15.

CHAPTER 11

Task Effectiveness
and Efficiency

As noted earlier, there are a number of tests of the quality of an environment for its users: is it pleasant, nondestructive, stimulating and vital, growth producing? One of the most obvious criteria (and indeed one that often drives out all the others in work organizations) is the appropriateness of a setting for the tasks performed there: does it help people do their work effectively and efficiently? Answering this question is basic to making effective design decisions.

ANALYZING PRODUCTIVITY-DESIGN RELATIONSHIPS

Despite its importance, trying to answer the question stated above is very difficult for several reasons. One is that there are only certain situations where you can make a one-to-one correspondence between settings' features and productivity of users, especially in the realm of office-type installations, which is the primary focus of this book. Many people have tried to "prove" that one environment or another is more productive, with clear success only in fairly limited efforts such as the reorganization of a typing area to provide a better paper flow or fewer distractions for the clerical staff. Even here it is not always clear whether social interactions are just distractions or are necessary breaks from alienating, repetitive tasks. So, even in such an apparently simple case there are complicating considerations. If the typists feel too cut off from one another, their concentration and output may be reduced even though they theoretically have fewer distractions. There seems to be an optimal level of contact for different people, and the setting can be structured just right or allow too little or too much interaction. It is an empirical question that needs to take actual employees into account, and is not amenable to a single "best" design solution.

Another cause of difficulty in tying environments directly to productivity is the looseness of the definition of "productivity" in office-type workplaces. Productivity can reasonably be measured by many indicators, such as the number of letters a group turns out per week; the amount of information they transmit in a timely manner to customers or other groups in the organization; the timeliness, number, and quality of decisions that a group makes; or the number of innovative products or services they develop. The answer to which measures to use is, "It all depends . . . " — on the organization's mission and primary goals, on the most crucial demands and expectations of the surrounding environment, and to some extent on the definitions of productivity that are preferred by the organization's top executives. They tend to define their own realities, since there are few absolute definitions. The key test is whether the managers' definitions of productivity will be positively related to the system's survival and accomplishment of its purposes for existing.

This ambiguous definition of office productivity is ironic when considered in the light of another aspect of settings management: managers who are asked to consider new forms of design or layout often demand clear-cut proof that the change will save them X dollars per year (seldom do they phrase it *make* X dollars per year). They do not seek a similar proof that their *present* environment is cost effective, nor do they seek it for many of the design choices they make regarding decorations, amenities, status symbols, and the like. In these cases they rely on their assumptions and beliefs — beliefs that such things are right, proper, and useful. But mention the notion of "productivity," and they switch into a "prove it to me or I will not buy it" mode. I suspect that this is often used as a means of avoiding consideration of alternatives that they intuitively do not like, or consideration of any change from the status quo, for that matter.

This leads to the last difficulty in linking office productivity levels directly with design of the physical setting. Many of the effects of settings on productivity come about indirectly, through their effects on other factors such as security, sense of identity, types of social interaction, and overall feel of the workplace to users. These factors, in turn, tend to produce climates that help people to work better at their tasks and to make better choices about which tasks are worth doing at all.[1]

In a sense, making effective design decisions in shaping a work setting requires one to be able to combine the many individual elements —

---

[1]For a discussion of the impact of physical settings on organizational climate, see F. Steele and S. Jenks, *The Feel of the Workplace* (Reading, Mass.: Addison-Wesley, 1977), ch. 8–9.

workplaces, furniture, layouts, traffic ways, colors, shared facilities, lighting — into larger wholes. One focus should be on a flow of experiences and influences on users, so that choices are made based on long- as well as short-term effects, and on the workings of the system as a whole as well as on activities of individuals or small groups considered independently. I do not believe that we as yet have good equations for making this assessment and expressing it in an easily applied manner. It requires a good deal of experience and a willingness to work on planning both organizational/social factors and physical factors concurrently, keeping in mind how each set is influencing the other. In Part II I tried to describe this back-and-forth process of physical and social structuring in enough detail to make it useful to readers as they create or alter their workplaces.

Having said at some length that it is difficult to tie environmental features directly to office productivity, there are still a number of influences or effects that are well enough known to be worth summarizing here. The rest of this chapter will suggest some key dimensions for thinking about these effects and some likely pitfalls to avoid. My goal is to help decisions about location, layout, decoration, density, graphics, furniture, and the like to be made based on a conscious view of the tasks actually being performed, the varieties of ways that users might perform them, and the more subtle effects of the settings on the performance of both individuals and the whole system.[2]

DEFINING TASKS AND PRODUCTIVITY

It is very hard to make good decisions about design and layout if you have not done a thorough job of describing what is to be done in the setting — what the tasks are now and how their emphasis will change over the life of the facility. This definition requires the help of people who are really doing the work. If it is done by just the top members of the system for everyone's areas, many of the real tasks that are crucial will be overlooked or underrated because they are far removed from the top leaders' experiences. I have seen facility layouts that you could take one look at and tell that they were done *for* the users by some higher manager who had not done the real work in many years. The users were always having to accommodate how they really did their work to the design, which

---

[2]A more detailed discussion of task settings can be found in F. Steele, *Physical Settings and Organization Development* (Reading, Mass.: Addison-Wesley, 1973), ch. 7; and in John Pile, "The Open Office: Does It Work?" *Progressive Architecture* 58 (June 1977): 68–81.

was based on an idealized image of how they ought to be doing the work. One corporate human resources group I know has instituted the opposite process. They utilize a self-diagnostic work analysis done by office groups who define their tasks and environmental needs themselves, then are helped to redesign work processes. This, in turn, leads naturally to a redesigning of the physical setting used to perform the work.

There are two main traps in this first step of defining tasks. One already mentioned is that the process can be dominated by top management who determine the answers without the requisite experiences; the other is a tendency for groups to skip over this question with a "that is obvious" attitude that leads them to traditional, mythical descriptions of their tasks based on old stereotypes. My hope is that managers can go beyond these to take a fresh look (as in the process of self-diagnosis) at what they *really* do, what they will be doing in the future, and how they could reorganize their work to do it better.

DESIGN DIMENSIONS AFFECTING PRODUCTIVITY

Relative Locations

Perhaps the most obvious design dimension affecting office productivity is one already considered in the social interaction chapter: the configuration of people, spaces, and equipment in relation to one another. Who is near whom, who is separated, and which facilities are easy and difficult to get to and use? Answers to all these questions affect the flow of information, paper, products, contacts, ideas, and the like, which is a good part of the work of an office installation. In order to make good choices about locations of people and things, one has to be clear about what needs to flow, and from where to where. What are the critical sequences that must happen easily and quickly in order for the primary tasks of the group to get done well? Is the flow one of paper, face-to-face contacts, physical products, or decisions and follow-up actions? Who really must be near whom, or near what equipment, in order that bottlenecks do not develop that slow down or confuse the overall flow?

One problem with this dimension is simply a lack of conscious attention to flow, especially in facilities that have been occupied for a long time. The layout eventually comes to be almost random, based on accumulated choices and changes that are now basically historical accidents, having little to do with today's work flow. The tendency is not to reexamine overall layout patterns until a move from the facility is planned, whereas it would make sense to periodically review relative locations and their impact on efficiency, just to check whether the facility is out-of-date. Another pitfall occurs when planning a new facility: doing an analysis of how information and contacts flow, and then designing layouts based on this analysis so that there is little consideration of how to improve this flow or how it will be changing over the next few years. That approach takes a static rather than a dynamic view of the system. A third complication is the political jockeying process in many organizations, where locational decisions are heavily influenced by self-oriented considerations of visibility, status, and political favor with powerful leaders. These factors are not wholly unrelated to subsequent productivity, but they often are a much stronger determinant of locational decisions than they ought to be from the point of view of task effectiveness.

Accessibility

The impact of locational decisions is made more or less crucial by another factor: the overall design's impact on *accessibility* of people to one another. Does the layout make it easy for people to see and interact with one another, and to be free not to interact when they do not want to? As discussed in Chapter 9, this issue could also be called "social interaction versus privacy" or "contact and stimulation versus withdrawal and concentration." Contact and isolation can each be more or less important and useful depending on the tasks being done and how they are structured. Layouts that file everyone away can dampen output when a group needs regular crossfertilization by members (or outsiders, for that matter). Layouts that force everyone to be in contact can dampen output when the tasks call for concentrated individual attention before useful sharing can occur.

This dimension becomes problematic when conflicts get shaped into single-answer moral stances: it is "good" for people to be working in contact with others all day, or it is "good" that everyone has a private workplace that is separate from everyone else's. The issue then becomes a battle over which position is the more ethical or correct. There is seldom a single answer to the interaction versus privacy issue, and some prior questions have to be asked and answered: Who are you talking about, what are their work styles, what kinds of tasks are they doing, what are the crucial actions that have to happen in order for the group to fulfill its mission, and how might the balance of needs for stimulation and concentration change with tasks or the times? It is unlikely that considering these questions will lead to one uniform answer to how accessible the layout should be. It is much more likely to require some variety of settings and some means of opening or closing contacts over time as users' needs change.

Differentiation and Integration

For an organization to achieve its mission and survive in its environment, it has to have certain structural properties. Among these are some differentiation among the parts of the system (so that they are not all doing the same thing all the time) and some integration of the parts (so that their activities are related to and support each other rather than going off in all directions). The degree of differentiation and integration needed in a given organization depends on the type of organization and the tasks done by it and its subunits. The optimum combination will also be affected by the stage of development of the organization, with differentiation being more important when groups are trying to develop an identity and style of their own, and integration being especially important during periods when the organization is trying to improve the interactions between its members and parts of its environment.

The system's physical facilities represent a key factor that can be manipulated in order to affect the system's degree of differentiation and integration. Differentiation of groups from one another can be emphasized by such moves as locating them in separate spots; using signs, symbols, and decorative elements that create distinctive "feels" or styles for groups; and designing controlled group areas and controlled access points so that people are aware of being inside or outside those areas. Integration is encouraged by actions such as locating groups near each other, with relative ease of contact and information sharing; creating central common areas that are identified with and used by more than one group; and designing efficient communication systems, both mechanical (e.g., telephone systems) and social (e.g., regular meetings).

From a physical design point of view, many office facilities seem to lack any clear model for what the appropriate levels of differentiation and integration are. Installations are built and occupied without clear goals on these dimensions, so that the impact tends to be random and not related to the needs of the system.

Size of Workplaces

An obvious design criterion for task efficiency is the size or scale of the work setting: is it large enough to allow the work to be done, but not so large that it is a waste of money and space? This issue can be looked at for an individual's workplace (e.g., are the work surfaces large enough for spreading out materials that people need to have in front of them in order to be doing their tasks effectively?) or for a whole group area (e.g., is it large enough to provide space for different activities such as impromptu meetings, or to allow people to function without being stressed from feeling overcrowded?). Once again, a general concept of appropriate scale for a particular work area should be derived from a clear image of the tasks to be done there, the climate to be created, and the styles of the particular people who will be using the facility. There are direct physical limits on activities if a space is too small; there are social costs (as well as economic) if a space is too small or too large (recall the case of a too-large setting being demoralizing because it reminded its users that they were the survivors from the firm's former days of glory). Size is a tricky dimension because the wrong-sized workplace may have its biggest impact in *hidden* costs — what people will tend not to do there (get together all the people who should be involved in a problem, display all the relevant information that should be seen in one place at one time, and so on) even though it looks like the day-to-day work is getting done.

This is one of the principal risks in determining the size of workplaces. There tends to be an overemphasis on visible, tangible dollar costs of the spaces and an underrepresentation of both the nontangible costs and gains associated with the size of workplaces. It is almost as if saving money on space was a measure of success, independent of its impact on accomplishing the primary tasks of the system. The organization is not in the business of minimizing space costs, any more than it would be considered to be a success by minimizing the cost of goods sold (COGS). The minimum COGS would be zero — by not making any products at all — but the system would have nothing to sell as a result of minimizing its costs and would therefore die for lack of fulfilling its purposes.

When it comes to space planning, the problems created by an overemphasis on up-front costs to the detriment of the gains of particular-sized spaces are increased if there is a lack of any clear model of how the system's tasks relate to its spaces — whether there is an organizational ecology focus that can include both quantitative and qualitative connections between settings and actions.

In most organizations the heavy emphasis on using the size of individual workplaces as a symbolic indicator of status or power in the organization is another major problem affecting design decisions. This is almost treated as a universal scale: more space means more status, and more status requires more space. The problem with this is that it can be uncorrelated (or even negatively correlated) with task needs for space, so that those whose tasks require spreading out have tiny spots and those who seldom require large areas or who are out traveling much of the time have huge offices designated as their exclusive turf. It has always been puzzling to me that stockholders will blithely accept this misallocation of system resources (from a functional point of view) apparently on the assumption that it is top management's right to overallocate space to themselves and shortchange those who need it for their tasks. To me this is an instance of mismanagement, but typical corporate norms say otherwise.

Symbolic Cues

My calling adherence to a rigid status symbol language mismanagement was not meant to dismiss the need for symbolic cues and information in an organization; these provide people with clues about where to go, what different groups are doing, and where people stand in the different groups and in the organization as a whole. This information helps to provide some predictability, so that many tasks can be done quickly without having to "reinvent the wheel" each time. Physical settings help or hinder these processes by being clear or blurry in their symbolic information, such as status symbols, group identification symbols, overall symbols of the mission and style of the organization, and individual touches that communicate about the style of individual persons. Again the prime question concerns which kinds of symbols help people to do their jobs, versus which are irrelevant or actually constraining but are holdovers from earlier norms and values in the organization. A system's symbols are usually a combination of current, helpful ones and old, outdated ones based on myths about what is important to the system. Additionally, this is not an easily discussed area, since many of these assumptions tend to be emotional and/or unconscious.

It may be risky for someone to raise the question of whether the symbolic language expressed in physical features is actually helping or hindering current and future work. The person who brings it up may be labeled as deviant or not fitting into those values that all good members should represent. In order to make this an area where choices can be made openly and consciously, an organization's top executives must take the lead in making the symbolism of settings a legitimate topic for analysis and choosing alternatives.

Flexibility

One of the biggest areas for concern in designing work settings today is that of flexibility — how to create workplaces that can be adapted to suit changing needs as tasks change in volume, scope, types of activities, and numbers of people who need to work closely with one another. Like other aspects of life today, the environment for work seems to be becoming more volatile and less predictable, so that designing a setting too specifically for one style of working will generally mean that it will rapidly become ill suited to the needs of its users. Even within this general trend toward greater volatility, however, there are still groups whose tasks change slowly and groups whose tasks change rapidly.

Determining how much and what kinds of flexibility need to be built into a work setting requires an analysis of the following factors: size of total space, sizes of individual spaces, relationships among workplaces (visible–not visible, close–distant), balance of private versus common areas, tightness of boundaries between groups, and so on. A lot of the push toward use of open-plan layout and furniture/screening systems as opposed to dry wall and traditional office furniture is based not on a love of this type of environment per se, but on the recognition that such a setting can be tinkered with quickly and at relatively low cost. More permanent settings require big decisions and will tend to be used unaltered even when they have become a detriment to day-to-day activities.

For example, John Pile presents a case of an advertising agency that switched to an open-plan layout:

> The other striking advantage that [the office's general manager] has exploited is the flexibility of open plan. Shortly after occupying the space, he instituted a general departmental reorganization in which the former, conventional functional organization was changed over to a project-team organization in which each team relates to the affairs of a particular client group and performs all functions for that group. This changeover took some time and was made in steps — a process that would have been extremely difficult in conventional space, but that was made painless by the flexibility of the open plan. Over a weekend, work stations could be arranged to accomplish an increment of change without significant loss of work time.[3]

The pitfalls in this area tend to be of two kinds. One is a lack of awareness of the whole dimension when settings are planned, which leads to building in unintentional rigidities that must be lived with for long periods or changed at great up-front costs. The other pitfall is related not to design but to *use* of settings. Flexibility is only an advantage if it is recognized and used. If there is a lack of informing and training managers in the possibilities of a new setting, they will tend to use it as if it were the older, more fixed type of environment. Similarly, if company policies and social norms make it difficult to take advantage of the flexibility that

---

[3]See John Pile, "The Open Office," 79.

is built in, it will tend to be underused and the setting will tend to deter task accomplishment as the times change.

SUMMARY

My purpose in selecting task definition, relative locations, stimulation, differentiation and integration, size of workplaces, symbolic cues, and flexibility as the key dimensions for a chapter on task effectiveness has been to suggest some of the questions that managers and groups should ask themselves when trying to create new workplaces or alter existing ones. The point is that if there is a norm of dealing openly with such dimensions, it is easier to manage conflicting priorities and needs. This in turn makes it more likely that the impact of a group's settings on their tasks will tend to be managed and positive, as opposed to accidental and often hindering. Open discussion of such ecological effects will also make it harder to engage in behind-the-scenes jockeying for power or territorial advantages, so that fewer key decisions will be made that unintentionally block the purposes of the organization while maintaining the status quo for selected individuals.

CHAPTER 12

Settings and Organizational Power and Influence

Everyone connected with workplace design and management knows that power and influence are facts of life in any human organization. Issues of status, power, control, participation, and freedom loom large in working out and implementing the design of office settings.

Power dynamics not only affect the design of work settings, but also are in turn affected by the features of settings and how those settings are used. The impact of physical settings on influence patterns is sometimes planned, sometimes accidental, but almost always a factor in shaping events and who influences them within the organization. This chapter will examine some of these effects in considering the following topics: settings as symbols of power and status, gaining power through the use of settings, settings as power elements in themselves, settings as an influence on events, physical features' effects on organizational dynamics, and some typical power problems related to organizational settings.

First we should consider a few general assumptions that underly much of the discussion in this chapter, so that readers will understand the origin of the views expressed here.[1]

"Organizational power" when used here means the ability to influence events in an organization in the directions you wish to. Power may be related to formal position in the system, although it is not synonymous with it.

Hard-and-fast rules about what something "means" in terms of physical indications of personal or group status in an organization are as likely

---

This chapter also appears in *Behavioral Issues in Office Design* (Jean D. Wineman, editor), published in 1986 by Van Nostrand Reinhold Company, Inc., New York.

[1]Some of the themes on power dynamics in organizations were influenced by my previously mentioned work with Barry Oshry. See his papers listed in chapter 10, note 1 and "The Success of a Business/The Failure of Its Partners."

to be wrong as right. Context and situation make a big difference, as does the history of how something got the way it is today.

In most organizations members tend to make frequent inferences about what physical symbols mean, and these inferences can cause problems by being overly rigid or self-serving.

Settings can be *indicators* of power differences and dynamics, *media* for influence and control, and *cues* for an observer diagnosing the dynamics and issues in a system.

Settings can be used consciously as a support for power moves, they may be used unconsciously to aid in influence or control, or they may influence events through patterns they cause, without any individual having chosen to do it.

To diagnose settings problems and potential from a human system point of view, you have to look at both how people make and alter places that help or hinder actions and how they use the settings that exist. The effects of settings are almost always a result of two complementary forces: the physical qualities of the place and the social system structure and norms of the people who are using it.

To repeat, I would like to counter a tendency for people to generate and believe in simplistic hard-and-fast rules about what an element of a setting "means" in power terms, or what one "must" do in order to be powerful in an organization. This area is more complex and deserves to be approached with some thoughtfulness and curiosity, rather than with dicta that usually hold true only when people with a lot of positional power can force them on those around them.

SETTINGS AS SYMBOLS OF POWER AND STATUS

One of the most familiar connections between settings and system dynamics is the manner in which messages are read into the places that different people and groups "own" or control within the organization. Being aware of these messages can help one be more sensitive to the roles that different individuals play in influencing people and events, as long as one is also aware of the limitations in this language. Symbolic messages are approximate, sometimes vague, often unintentional (unplanned), and can mean more than one thing at the same time. As already cautioned, it is important not to make too many inferences without getting some confirmation from other sources.

With this in mind, we will examine a few of the dimensions or qualities that are used in our culture to symbolize a person's or a group's power in an organization.

Luxury Features and Trappings

A common indicator of organizational status is luxuriousness of a setting: fine materials, comfortable furniture, expensive accessories, large spaces, high-quality art works, and so on. Whether or not these are indicators of power in the organization is a different story, however. One has to know more about the situation, since there are cases where status and power are not synonymous. For instance, a senior executive may be provided with a plush office but given very little to do (being "put out to pasture"). He or she has been given trappings in lieu of the power to really influence events in the organization.

There are also settings where luxury does mean power, at least the power to provide oneself with fine things when others cannot make that choice. The executive who takes such action often justifies it as being expected of someone in that position ("I really don't care myself") or necessary to functioning in a high-powered mode ("It sets a tone that helps me exert authority"). This may or may not be the actual effect, but the argument justifies the luxurious surroundings.

Locations

There are different messages associated with different locations in an organization. Closeness to the acknowledged power center (person or group) is used as one measure. There is some justification for this, since those who are close are more likely to have regular contact with the top people, and to have been chosen for such contact. Locations near the highest activity areas are another type of indicator. Many personnel departments are seen as low in power, which is consistent with their backwater locations away from crucial management action. If they agree to be placed there, they are colluding in reducing their own perceived (and real) clout in the system.

Location of one's workplace within a given area can also carry messages about power. The usual factors have to do with being near the boss, near a window, near a corner, or on the way to important people but not too accessible (e.g., executive-row layouts).

In a given building, location by floor level is sometimes an indicator of standing in the competitive sweepstakes. Simple height off the ground is a surprisingly common indicator, with career progress being measured by how high up in the building one has risen. This is thrown haywire when a new boss decides that he or she wants to move down to the ground floor to be more visible to the troops. It makes sense to them as an experiment and may increase their sense of what is happening in the system, but it confuses all the middle management people who have faithfully played the climbing-the-building game. The norm has been defied and is no longer to be completely relied upon.

Security

Keys, locks, doors, barriers, and other control devices can indicate power for those who control their use. You can sometimes measure the importance of an executive by the number of tests one has to pass in order to get access to the executive, such as how many doors to pass through or how many receptionists to be satisfied by your credentials.

A door does not have to be closed in order for its owner to be seen as powerful — it just has to be available for the closing and be seen as controlled at the person's discretion.

Seating in Meetings

A common power indicator is the location of people's seats in meetings of all kinds, from small staff meetings to large conference center gatherings of whole departments or larger collections. The messages here are harder to state unequivocally, but they tend to relate to three areas: where one chooses to sit, where one is allowed or instructed to sit, and group norms about who should sit where in a given event. Location around a meeting conference table is probably the simplest example, with nearness to the boss being a measure of standing in the meeting. This may be misleading, however, since a relatively equal rival may choose to sit opposite the boss as a way of highlighting the tension between the two of them. That is a high-impact location in terms of getting the boss's attention (and easier to make eye contact than a side-by-side position), even though it is not typically thought of as a high-status one. The most extreme examples are at formal events such as stockholders' meetings, with the inside power people sitting at the front of the room on a raised platform and everyone else sitting as the "audience" (e.g., passive receivers of leaders' pronouncements), although activist stockholders may not accept this expected passive role no matter where they are seated.

In sum, there are a number of qualities that are part of the language of power standing in an organization. Some of these are typical of most systems (e.g., luxurious trappings), and some are particular to a given organization (such as a particular building whose history in the development of the firm makes it *the* place to have one's office). They all have an element of the self-fulfilling prophecy about them. When people believe that a person's setting speaks of power, they tend to treat them with more deference and concern, thus conceding them more power and influence. It is sometimes hard to know which direction the influence is taking—does a person acquire power symbols because of his or her clout, or does the person acquire clout as his or her power symbols increase? One thing that we should always keep in mind is that there are no universal messages that are always sent by a given setting. Hard-and-fast interpretations, when I hear them in an organization, usually have a self-serving element, since it is to the interpreter's advantage that a particular arrangement be thought of as having only one possible interpretation.

POWER ACQUIRED THROUGH MODES OF USING SETTINGS

Another interesting effect on power relations in settings comes not from *what* the setting is like but from how it is *used*. There is usually great latitude for using settings to enhance one's power, influence, or dramatic impact. Some people are quite good at consciously choosing options to achieve desired effects. For instance, if there is a choice of possible settings for a crucial meeting that is likely to be confrontational, you can try to have the meeting be in your home territory so that you can legitimately play the role of host or hostess, while the others are cast in the role of guests. This is not the only role influence in the session, but it is a factor that might as well be working for you as against you.

People who use settings for influence are usually more likely to make conscious choices about where events should be held, whereas those who are not so aware of this process tend to take what is available or usual as their scenes for events. (In a small survey of consultants, most had not thought much about where they chose to do different activities or even about what processes they used for choosing sites.)

During an event in a given setting, there are influence moves that people make by where they place themselves in the setting. If everyone is sitting down, it can be useful to remain standing as a way of differentiating yourself from the rest. And, vice versa, if everyone is standing, I have seen a person gain the spotlight by being the only one sitting down. Where one places oneself in a room can have a similar effect: under a light, at a corner position that draws people's eyes, near a door that is the only entrance or exit, at the "head" of the table (if there is an obvious spot like that), and so on. One thing that should be remembered is that there is no single rule, such as always to be standing or sitting to control attention. It depends on the situation, the structure of the setting, and a person's goals.

A similar process is one I have dubbed "the positive power of puttering." This is the use of props in a setting to focus attention, draw out the conversation, or control the flow of time and pace of the event. An obvious example is the way a pipe smoker will begin a statement and then putter with the relighting of his pipe while still maintaining a claim to the floor. If done well, he can control the total pace of the conversation that way. Similar moves can be made with almost anything that is handy in a setting: pointers, flip chart pads, coffee cups and pots, magazines, or whatever. Anything can be used to putter with and draw attention to a particular person or spot at a particular time, often without others' being aware of the way their attention is focused by the moves. Even standing up and pacing in a conference room at a crucial moment is a way of puttering with the available free space and one's feet.

These considerations also suggest that a setting that has a lot of "stuff" in it is richer in puttering possibilities than one that does not. One thing that provides high-power bosses with extra clout when they hold meetings in their own offices is that they have a lot of their own things to trifle with during the meeting, and it is legitimate for them to do it but would be considered rude for visitors to do the same. An office that is very thin in personal items is a harder setting in which to do this, from the owner's point of view, and is a meager contribution to attention focusing and dramatic moves.

SETTINGS AS POWER ELEMENTS THEMSELVES

Our next topic concerns situations in which a setting is not just a symbol or message, it is a power element in and of itself. In such a case, the setting has the power to influence the behavior of users, and those who understand this will use that quality to their own advantage. Settings are often consciously set up to be a means of control, so that managers will not have to make visible influence attempts personally. For example, signs with rules and instructions are displayed visibly so that persons who are responsible (or feel responsible) for seeing that these rules are obeyed will not have to speak to each person who comes in and explain the rules. And, if they should see someone disobeying the rules, they can merely point to the sign, as if to say, "It has nothing to do with me, the rules are right there for all to see."

Another example is less tangible but no less powerful. The history of a particular setting sometimes builds an atmosphere that controls the behavior of people who use the setting. A board room may have been the setting for famous events that people recall each time they use it for a meeting, just as Yankee Stadium is a potent setting for many baseball players since so much of the history of American baseball has happened there.

Settings are also designed to have selective power over certain categories of users. The most obvious example is the typical courtroom, which is structured to exert considerable power over defendants and other noninsiders (such as the audience) while allowing a fair amount of freedom for the insiders (such as the judge, police, clerks, and lawyers).

Territorial boundary markers create a certain type of power for settings, mainly that of allowing or blocking movement or access between parts of an organization. An office complex with most groups hidden away behind blank doors has an almost tangible power over employees' movement between groups. It will usually stifle movement, except in times of high stress when people feel they need to see others face-to-face. Then the layout requires a lot more movement than would another plan. When people cannot see from their own spot whether someone else is in, they must move through the doors and find out, often repeating this three or four times until they make the connection. Visibility in a setting can therefore be a powerful control medium, depending on who is visible to whom. The classic example of this is the open bull-pen arrangement in the old-style insurance office, with all desks in rows facing the same direction and the supervisor on a slightly raised platform at the back where he or she can see everyone without being observed.

Settings also have a kind of power through literally providing a place to be, a structure in space so that one can function for a period of time without having to worry about finding a legitimate spot. This is power of a sort, but it is usually taken for granted by most of us until, for one reason or another, we get into a powerless situation where we have no place to go. Then we realize how forlorn we feel without a setting in which to operate freely as ourselves.

An interesting organizational example of this phenomenon was observed at an interservice military training institute that occupies space on a large, permanent base. The institute has approximately 150 students per program, most of whom live on the base. These students have no community place designated as their own within the institute's territory on the host base. They are either in the main classroom (the auditorium), in discussion rooms (in the administration building), or wandering on the base. They have no place to gather and spend time at the institute. This condition is both disempowering and hinders their developing any shared identity as a group. It also tends to keep them uninfluential in relation to the staff of the institute. The system pays a price in terms of its product, since the shape and content of the program will tend to be influenced mostly by the staff and very little by the students. If the students had a common space where they could get together and talk about what was going on and how they liked or did not like it, they would be more likely to develop a common consciousness of their position and of the possibilities of influencing the staff if they took concerted action. It is doubtful that the staff would *want* this to happen, though; the present layout rather suggests that they would not. But there are still high costs to the system because program content can become unrealistic without being challenged. The layout tends to skew influence distribution in favor of the staff, not the students, so the students tend to remain a collectivity rather than becoming a group with a shared identity and perceptions of similar concerns, interests, and rights.

SETTINGS AND EVENTS

A special case of the power of settings is the way that they can influence the character of particular events in an organization. We previously noted that layouts with groups close to or distant from one another have an effect on the interaction patterns of the two groups and help determine whether they get together to discover common interests and concerns. Similarly, when a crisis hits an organization, it is a different event if the system is laid out in an open plan than if everyone is dispersed in private offices that are hidden from one another. The news travels much faster in the open plan. The mood of the place can be affected in a day, and one can see that mood change in the way others are moving about or talking with one another. This is not to say that one layout is better than the other — that depends on how fast a manager wants a mood to spread and the capacity of the members of a group to respond to the crisis without panicking.

Another example of a setting influencing events is the conference area that is very tight for space with overlapping group areas impinging on it. Meetings to diagnose problems of one group, when held there, may be much more constrained than they would be in a more private space with no fear of being overheard. The whole feel of the session would be different and less public oriented.

Where events are held influences power balances and the overall tenor of events, especially regularly recurring ones. In one major corporation's large manufacturing complex (made up of several smaller factories), all meetings held by the complex's manager with his staff were held in the conference room of the administration building. This room was next to the complex manager's office and across the hall from those of the personnel and finance managers. The department heads of the different plants (who came from their own areas for the meetings) seemed to take little interest in the discussions of site-wide issues, and most of the talking was done by the complex manager and the personnel and finance managers.

It seemed that this pattern might partly be caused by holding all the meetings in the territory of the most talkative threesome. This may have explained why they were the most talkative — they were in their home turf and therefore more comfortable than the operations managers. As an experiment, we switched the meetings to a rotation to different locations around the complex, so that different people hosted it on different weeks. It became a much more lively meeting, with the plant managers becoming more verbal about common issues in the complex. They had not changed, but their feelings about themselves in the meeting were more positive. This strategy also gave the complex manager much more of a feel for what was happening around the complex, versus the view from his own administration building. The personnel and finance managers became less talkative but more interested in what the others had to say and in what was going on in other areas.

The nature and level of lighting can also have a great effect on the character of an event, no matter what the intentions of the people who set it up. Lighting can make the mood intimate (if low), public (if bright), festive (if varied and playful), and so on. Spotlights can focus attention on one or more people; turning on the house lights in a theater can raise audience members' awareness of themselves and their numbers. The possibilities of variable lighting are often underutilized in organizations as a device to shape events.

The symbolic messages that settings hold can influence specific events as well as people's perceptions of the influence of others. An example is the board room with pictures of the company's founders around the walls, which is also used as a conference and training room. The pictures carry a high message value about continuity, permanence, stability, and traditional values of the organization. This setting can be perfect for certain traditional events, but it can also set a tone of conservatism and stability that makes it very hard to explore new directions or to get people to think for themselves about what the system could be like in the future. The walls say "follow the people and norms that made us what we are today," and the pressure is on not to look ungrateful for this past leadership by rejecting what they stood for.

Finally, the weather can be a major force shaping the pattern of what can occur in a setting. If the weather is cold and icy, outdoor rallies are usually disappointing. If the weather is hot and sticky, outdoor meetings may degenerate into lethargic get-togethers (as many training directors have found after scheduling winter conference sessions in Florida or the Bahamas). It is a nice experience, but not much energy gets brought to bear on the issues. Bad weather can also be a catalyst, as when it spurs people who control no sheltered workplaces of their own to come together to demand more from the "haves." In a good climate, people can get by with fewer resources, so their threshold of frustration tends to be higher, or slower to be reached.

SETTINGS AND HUMAN SYSTEMS DYNAMICS

The effects we have been considering here can be viewed through another interesting angle, which is the impact of physical setting features on the dynamic events and behaviors taking place in an organization. This is particularly relevant since power was defined at the start of this chapter as the ability to influence organizational events in desired directions.

Since the number of possible effects to consider is enormous, I have summarized them in Table 12.1, which provides examples of the typical impact of six physical feature categories of office settings on twelve areas of organizational dynamics and behavior, which may be described as follows:

1. *Boundary management.*   The kinds of controls that people exert over the movement of people, information, money, materials, and so on among organizational units and between the organization and its environment
2. *Energy management.*   The stimulation and direction of human energy to various activities and ends (not to be confused with physical energy management, such as heat and lighting costs)
3. *Controlling resources.*   The use of various desirable resources (money, information, one's own time, and so on) to produce something or influence events
4. *Positional behavior.*   The influence of people's positions (social and physical) on their behaviors and on others' perceptions of them
5. *Controlling structures.*   The influencing of the various formal (responsibility and reporting relationships) and informal (casual groupings, temporary teams) structures that influence behavior in the system

Table 12.1
Examples of the Effects of
Physical Setting Features on
Organizational Behavior

Physical Features	Organizational Dynamics	
	1. Boundary Management	2. Energy Management
(A) Locations of offices, depart- ments, desks, etc.	° adjacency increases contact ° distance decreases it ° visibility leads to less mystery ° choice of mixing vs. separat- ing units ° dispersal vs. concentration changes experience pattern	° visibility of action can make enthusiasm contagious ° hassle factor if separation distance is large ° overcrowding⟶stress⟶tension tension⟶action ? ° communication equipment needs
(B) Design of entrances, exits, and accessways	° clear vs. hidden access ° "insider" - "outsider" feel if hidden or difficult ° visitors' first experience ° possible visual distractions ° controlling access -- easy or difficult	° distractions break concentration ° channeling people to right place without energy drain ° regular outside inputs can stimulate thought and action
(C) Furniture arrangements	° defining areas with furniture arrangements ° a "screening person" must be in right spot ° furniture styles can sharpen differences among group	° making easy visual and audial contact possible ° having right type and size of furniture for tasks ° visibility tends to promote sense of common concerns ° controlling interferences with productive work
(D) Signs and other graphics	° "enter" or "keep out" messages control access ° help in finding access or exits ° temporary signs to open or close boundaries ° styles in decorations and art works for units	° visual reminders of issues or concerns needing action ° directing people to right place for their purposes ° posted rules about activity accepted or not ° stimulating vs. soothing colors
(E) Trafficways, aisles, and corridors	° may need to block a path to close a boundary ° passing through a group's area or to the side ° are there easy links between groups?	° paths affect energy needed to get from A to B ° different modes of movement possible with different path ° with easy movement, people can pass excitement on to others (vs. dissipate)
(F) Lighting arrangements and level	° different intensities can signal different zones ° dark spots often act as a barrier to free movement ° different styles of fixtures identify groups' areas	° different light levels tend to stimulate energy or reduce it ° dimness or glare can induce fatigue in high-concentration tasks

Table 12.1 (cont.)

Physical Features	Organizational Dynamics	
	3. Controlling Resources	4. Positional Behavior
(A) Locations of offices, depart- ments, desks, etc.	° doling out high-quality, high-status locations ° deciding who can be where and what can be done in different locations ° determining adjacencies and therefore opportunities	° being in a spot where one doesn't see what's happening ° being ceded authority because of one's location ° department members' concern for certain issues because their location induces certain experiences
(B) Design of entrances, exits, and accessways	° who has access to resources (stock room, computer, copier, etc.) ° are resources visible or hidden? ° access to facilities at non-standard times may be tightly controlled	° people tend to be put in space-guardian role due to location of their work spot (e.g., secretary near a door) ° role expectations set by cues from entrances and exits
(C) Furniture arrangements	° variations in what items one has to work with ° formal rules about accept-able arrangements ° control harder without visibility of what you are trying to control	° certain arrangements (and there-fore work modes) that are supposed to go with a position ° desk arrangements which increase/decrease visible activity (and awareness)
(D) Signs and other graphics	° control of graphics - degree of personal choice ° signs which delineate owner-ship of facilities ° signs which declare who can use what	° indicators of position and status in the system ° titles, names and functions displayed directly ° informal status language: type and quality of art, decorative arrangements, etc.
(E) Trafficways, aisles, and corridors	° path control helps control access to stuff ° who can use which paths (such as executor elevator) can shape what people can do easily ° freedom of movement is a resource itself	° people may skip making face-to-face contact because path is muddled or difficult ° people on trafficways often seem irritable, due to pattern of interruptions (not to personality)
(F) Lighting arrangements and levels	° making an area unlighted restricts its use ° power people can program lighting patterns over the course of a day if there is a centrally controlled system	° lighting arrangements appropriate to one's position may be poor for one's work style preference ° personal task lighting choices vs. uniform general lighting affect choices about different work modes at different times

Table 12.1 (cont.)

Physical Features	Organizational Dynamics	
	5. Controlling Structures	6. Differentiation of Units
(A) Locations of offices, depart- ments, desks, etc.	° configurations often deter- mine where events can be held, or if they can ° being located centrally can help one see patterns and know when to let go of old structure/create new	° very different types of locations tend to sharpen differences between groups ° people can move their desks away to make statement about differentiation
(B) Design of entrances, exits, and accessways	° are entrances right for flow when important meetings are held? Are exits right? ° Groups may play different functions based on their access to other groups	° clear exclusion of some groups from contact with others ° insiders-outsiders set-up sharpens differences ° groups may use poor access as an issue to establish separate identity
(C) Furniture arrangements	° setting up special arrange- ments to control the flow of meetings, conferences and the like ° setting rules about arrange- ments, as a means to con- rolling relationships	° different styles of layout signal group differences in outlook, values, etc. ° furnishings for a whole building may be uniform, to minimize difference, or tailored to different groups to heighten it
(D) Signs and other graphics	° rules, constraints and pro- cedures visibly displayed ° are there clear messages in right places about expectations for events?	° identifying signs for groups' territories ° banners used to identify group areas (in open-plan layouts) ° distinctive decorative elements, colors, etc.
(E) Trafficways, aisles, and corridors	° rules about who can use which paths, and when ° creating new paths can help create new bonds between formerly separate groups or individuals	° passageways tend to separate groups when they run between them ° lack of a path joining two groups tends to accentuate differences
(F) Lighting arrangements and levels	° controlling policies about lighting (type, time of use, etc.) can shape which events can occur and when	° differences in style or intensity set different moods for different groups ° big difference/contrast in lighting level tends to sharpen awareness of different group territories

Table 12.1 (cont.)

Physical Features	Organizational Dynamics	
	7. Integration of Units	8. Face-to-Face Influence
(A) Locations of offices, departments, desks, etc.	° putting uni·s in same building ° mixing-up groups, not totally separate location ° adjacency with easy access ° communication equipment when distances are great	° adjacency provides unplanned moments of contact and influence ° being central allows one to be around and act when an issue is hot
(B) Design of entrances, exits, and accessways	° inviting entrance to a group's area can draw others for better communication ° clear access speeds contact in emergencies	° designs can control who has access to power people and who gets a chance to influence them ° choices of exits from an office or area allow people to escape face-to-face contact if not desired
(C) Furniture arrangements	° workplaces arranged for easy sharing of information ° trading of items among group ° similar settings that make members of different groups feel comfortable	° an office set up to place resident in dominant mode over visitors (imposing desk, light source behind resident, poor seating for visitor, etc.) ° visibility of subordinates to boss
(D) Signs and other graphics	° integrated decoration of system ° signs encouraging visits from one group to another ° maps and charts showing locations and paths for different groups' areas	° visible instructions about who to see for various pieces of business ° certificates, plaques, etc. displayed at personal workplaces to establish credibility
(E) Trafficways, aisles, and corridors	° paths can link groups together, absence of clear paths encourages independent actions	° trafficways provide settings for impromptu chats and influence (if they are wide enough to allow stopping and chatting) ° visible, open paths allow one to spot passersby
(F) Lighting arrangements and level	° common lighting systems or patterns tend to tie groups together ° common switches or controls require groups to coordinate decisions about lighting	° level of lighting can set mood of intimacy, conspiracy, public posturing, etc. ° lighting can focus people's attention on each other or on surroundings

Table 12.1 (cont.)

Physical Features	Organizational Dynamics	
	9. Symbolic Messages	10. Controlling Events
(A) Locations of offices, departments, desks, etc.	° who's up/down in status shown by location ° some locations hold more territorial messages than others do (based on the system's history) ° closeness to power centers (e.g., president's office) implies standing	° putting people near one another can spark issues or confrontations ° high densities of people in same area can raise tensions and aggression ° holding events in your own turf can provide control over them
(B) Design of entrances, exits, and accessways	° thoughtfulness of entrances and exits says something about welcomeness of visitors ° design implies who counts, who doesn't in the system	° access can be used as an issue to draw people together to take common action ° entrances shape how people get to events, and how they feel at the start
(C) Furniture arrangements	° seating arrangements tell others about one's desired interpersonal style ° style of furnishings may reflect personal style ° layouts imply what activities are OK in a setting	° set-ups for meetings, conferences, etc. shape the processes that can happen ° special arrangements are institutionalized to control events (e.g., courtrooms) ° layout scheme affects contact (e.g., open vs. closed layout)
(D) Signs and other graphics	° status indicators such as titles, colors, etc. ° taste in art may be communicated if occupant chose it ° basic functions of different groups shown by graphics in their areas	° can be visible messages which set mood, influence awareness and feelings ° can create zones or areas with graphics -- special spots for special events
(E) Trafficways, aisles, and corridors	° freedom of use of different paths is sign of insider or power status ° freedom from trafficways in own area can also be a sign of high status (one rates an enclave)	° the movement of people, spontaneous gatherings, chance meetings are all influenced by the structure of paths and access ° shutting off access to paths can keep events from happening
(F) Lighting arrangements and level	° lighting level sets a mood, speaks about nature of contact that someone desires ° being nearer to natural light often taken as sign of higher status	° climate and mood of an event influenced by nature and intensity of light ° light can focus members' attention (e.g., a spotlight)

Table 12.1 (cont.)

Physical Features	Organizational Dynamics	
	11. Physical Coercion	12. Subunit Power
(A) Locations of offices, depart- ments, desks, etc.	° placing people so they are visible to the controller ° secure locations that cannot be entered without identi- fication or keys ° isolated locations that make users dependent on authority figures	° powerful units tend to be in central spots where they can easily get and give information ° locations that were chosen by the group often reflect power just through the freedom to choose
(B) Design of entrances, exits, and accessways	° entrances can be blocked and exits as well, so that they are only usable when controller decided ° fortifications designed so access can only be gained through entrances	° careful entrances provide units control of their own turf ° entrances within a group area can provide members with freedom of movement, build self-esteem
(C) Furniture arrangements	° jail cells and work cubicles both imply rules about re- stricted movement ° freedom to choose arrange- ments (or lack of it) is communicated by settings to those who can read them	° the typical facilities manage- ment group controls other groups' actions by setting policies about use of furniture and space ° power images may be projected by style and placing of furnishings
(D) Signs and other graphics	° visual directives about per- mitted and forbidden actions ° warnings, visual reminders of past punishments, etc.	° clear strong identity may be projected by the graphics in a group's area ° directives to steer unwanted traffic away or draw desired traffic through a group's area
(E) Trafficways, aisles, and corridors	° degree of security (walls, fences, etc.) determines their usability ° paths that are busy may be safer than those that are isolated	° locations near many paths or nodes tend to strengthen a unit's power; backwater locations tend to reduce it
(F) Lighting arrangements and level	° spotlights in areas where surveillance is desired ° light as a weapon, as in "the 3rd degree" ° ability to cut off light source	° power is indicated by which groups have the right to deviate from standard system or set up one of their own

6. *Differentiation of units.* Sharpening differences of style, responsibility, capability, and so on among the various units of the organization
7. *Integration of units.* The connections of the units to one another through information sharing, coordination of actions, joint decisions, and so on
8. *Face-to-face influence.* People attempting to influence each other's opinions, ideas, or readiness to act, and doing this when physically in each other's presence
9. *Symbolic messages.* The large mass of information that is communicated in the organization in an informal manner through signs, symbols, and other graphics
10. *Controlling events.* Trying to shape the occurrence, nature, or sequence of events that occur within the system
11. *Physical coercion.* Influencing people's behavior in the organization by physical threats or constraints
12. *Subunit power.* The relative ability of an organizational unit to influence other parts of the system and shape events

The six physical feature categories that I have selected for illustration are

A. Locations of offices, departments, desks, and so on
B. Design of entrances, exits, and accessways
C. Furniture arrangements
D. Signs and other graphics
E. Trafficways, aisles, and corridors
F. Lighting arrangements and level

In Table 12.1 each cell contains examples of the effects of the particular physical feature on the particular category of organizational behavior. This is not meant to be a complete survey but rather to suggest patterns that readers can look for in their own organizations or take into account when designing new office settings.

SUMMARY

This chapter has attempted to explore some of the many aspects of the relationships between organizational influence and power dynamics with various aspects of the organization's settings: how they are structured, the impact they have on events in the organization, how they are used as a power language, who can use them in what ways, and who has the power to shape them for their own purposes. This is a very complex area that is not amenable to simple rules about what elements always mean or what one must do in order to exercise desired influence through physical facilities. This topic cannot adequately be summed up in a single short chapter, therefore my intention has been to provide some themes to help readers look at the relationships (actual and potential) between physical settings and power dynamics in their own organizations.

We can say with some certainty that positional power, perceived power, influence over events, and control over the shape and use of facilities are inextricably bound with each other, so that anyone who wants to improve the functioning of their organization by improving the match of physical and social structures needs to be able to look at these factors in a clear, open-minded, problem-solving manner. The process cannot be overly dependent on old interpretations and solutions, or it will be manipulated by whoever in the system wants to play the territory-and-trappings game for their own particular ends.

One of the most important issues to keep in mind when trying to cut through such games is the difference between focusing on getting the facilities one personally wants as an individual (e.g., a certain type of workplace, furniture, location) and focusing on the facilities that the organization needs in order to function effectively (e.g., how many separate workspaces and how many combined ones). My observations suggest that once most managers get past rudimentary choices such as size of total office area and overall layout, they tend to deal with facilities design issues as the sum of individuals' concerns (including their own). While these concerns are important, facilities design decisions and use patterns could be improved by also spending time on the effects of design choices on the health and power dynamics of the organization and its subgroups.

These effects are not the same as summing up how satisfied individuals are with their own workplaces and with the overall decorative style. Individuals need to have some degree of satisfaction with their personal workplaces or their resentment will block productive work in the long run, but this satisfaction is not a sufficient condition of organizational health. Poor layouts from the point of view of the organization's patterns of action may occur even while most individuals like their workplaces. Designers and users must remain aware of both personal and systemic effects in order to create settings that influence power behavior and other organizational dynamics in a positive manner.

CHAPTER 13

The Impact of Settings
on Boundary Relations

The previous chapter touched on one of the aspects of social structure that gives the most definitive shape to organizational life: the boundaries between parts. "Boundaries" as we will use the term here refers to the nature of separations both between groups within the organization and between the organization as a whole and its surrounding social and physical environment. Boundaries define where one entity stops and another begins. Physical features of a setting are often used to define such a boundary (e.g., this side of the wall is our territory and that side of the wall is theirs). They also influence the ways in which groups manage their boundary relationships with other people and groups, making it easier or more difficult to control such relations, such as when a group is trying to keep nonmembers from coming into their space but there are too many access points to be controlled easily. There are two types of boundary management features: physical elements such as walls, doors, and gates that can be opened or closed to physically open or close boundaries; and symbolic features that attempt to change people's psychological awareness of boundaries and influence whether or not they want to cross them in the first place (decorative elements, signs, graphics, and the like).

While examining some of the main effects of settings on boundary relations in an organization, we should keep in mind that there is no universal answer as to what boundary relations should be like between two groups in an organization. Sometimes the health of the organization and the respective missions of the groups would suggest that they should have a loose, "permeable" boundary that allows an easy flow of people, ideas, materials, and information between them. In other cases it would serve the organization as a whole (and the mission of each group) better if they have a relatively tight boundary that acts to keep them more separate. As times change, the need for a tight boundary may also give way to the need for a more open one, or vice versa.

Since there is no universal answer to what boundary relations should be like, this becomes a diagnostic question that can only be answered by considering the needs of the groups and the organization at a specific phase of their development. It is also a question that definitely should be asked when physical facilities are planned, so that the impact of these facilities is consistent with the boundary relationships an organization is trying to create or maintain.

We will turn now to a discussion of the ways in which the physical setting influences or shapes boundary relations, including relations among groups within an organization, boundary relations between headquarters and field locations, and relations between an organization and the different parts of its environment.

BOUNDARY EFFECTS BETWEEN GROUPS

There are many possible examples of the effects of physical elements on boundary relations within an organization. One of the most powerful is also one of the most obvious: the relative location of groups has a large impact on how easy it is for them to have contact, share information and experiences, be able to step in and provide help for one another on short notice, and so on. Sheer distance plays a big part in this — the shorter the distance between two groups, the more likely the boundary is to be permeable, other things being equal. There is also a special impact associated with whether or not the two groups are located under the same roof, in the same building, or in buildings that are clearly differentiated. Even if the actual distance between buildings is quite small (such as twenty or thirty feet), the boundary separation tends to be quite marked, since the arrangement increases everyone's awareness of the differences between the groups.

For example, in Chapter 12 I mentioned the case of an interservice military training institute located on a "host" base. Because the institute had to create spaces however it could, all the administrative staff were housed in one building, and all the academic faculty/discussion leaders were in another building across a narrow street. There tended to be a lot of friction between the two staffs, relatively little crossgroup information sharing, and a good deal of mutual resentment (especially by the teaching staff of the administrative group). There were many unresolved power issues concerning control of personnel matters, student affairs, and the overall directions of the institute. These issues were not strictly speaking *caused* by the separateness of the physical layout; they are common in educational institutions because of the conflicting interests of faculty and administration. But they were exacerbated by the two-building layout and certainly not helped toward being resolved.

In other words, there was a very tight boundary between faculty and administrative groups. This was likely to get even tighter if the structure remained the same. When I was there, the faculty group was planning to turn one of their rooms into a lounge for their own exclusive use, which would further tighten the boundary. (They were sharing a common lounge area with the administration, but they resented the fact that it was across the street.) The original decision to place the groups in separate buildings was made primarily because the numbers of people fit well into each building. This decision ignored the continuing impact that such a layout would have on boundary relations. Once such a decision has been made (more or less unconsciously), it becomes harder and harder to change, since the people in each group feel more and more identified with their own group and its turf, and more distance from and dissimilarity with the other group. Because of this trend, I believe that it is a tougher problem to change from a tight-boundary, high-separation structure toward looser boundaries than it is to move from a loose-boundary physical layout toward a tighter one.

There are, of course, many other physical features that affect subgroup boundary relations in an organization. Sheer visibility is also an influence in the separate buildings case: when groups see each other coming and going, they are more likely to be aware of each other's style, needs, problems, and so on. This will generally reduce barriers between the groups unless their styles are *so* different that the members of one group are only made aware of these differences and it makes them feel that the others are definitely a world apart. That situation usually builds up pressure for a physical change so that the groups are no longer so visible to each other and therefore not such a source of tension.

Another key element is really a *pattern* of elements: the design of *entrances* and *exits* to groups' areas. These may be clear, inviting, ambiguous, or menacing. The first two types tend to promote easy boundary contacts, and the second two to encourage separation through the use of locked doors, small openings that require a pass or identification in order to pass through, or an entrance with a person stationed nearby to screen unacceptable people. Related to entrances are *traffic features*: where groups are located with respect to aisles, walkways, corridors, and such. Placement of these determines whether a group's area will generally have a lot of passers-through from other groups or almost no one coming into its area except specific visitors. In groups open to through traffic, the members will find it harder to control their boundaries with other groups, since their activities, decorations, comings and goings, notices on boards, and the like will all be relatively public information. To operate in a more private mode, the group may have to block off some formerly familiar trafficways altogether, thereby closing up the boundary with other groups. There is a problem that can arise when doing this. In trying to keep out certain groups, the group may also send a signal to "stay out" to other groups with which it still needs regular contact. Closing boundaries selectively is difficult and requires careful planning.

One of the solutions that is often used for doing this kind of selective boundary tightening is a system of *signs and graphics* that provide clear information about where a group's area begins, who is allowed in there (or not), where one should go in order to enter in the correct manner, and what particular rules exist about behavior while in that area. A "members only" or "employees only" sign is a very simple tight-boundary mechanism, although if nonmembers are not easily deterred it will not work by itself. Some sort of physical control (e.g., a locked door or gate) or human screen (e.g., a guard on duty) will be needed to keep the boundary secure from intrusions. In the extreme, there are work groups that send so many control signals that they feel like an elite private club to nonmembers, and their ability to get information about what is going on in the rest of the organization suffers as a result. The general point, though, is that a group is more likely to get desired messages across to other people about when it is and is not all right to visit if they set some conscious goals about boundary relations and use signs and graphics to communicate information in a straightforward manner. Subtle hints may have been the usual mode, but they are less likely to get the message across effectively.

Another factor in subunit boundary relations is the *pattern of decorative elements* in groups' areas: whether there are visible personal touches, the style of furnishings and arrangements, the nature of colors and materials used, and so on. A pattern is a very effective way to differentiate one area from another, and it is often used in an open-plan layout as a substitute for solid walls and doors. Considered in this light, there is a real cost to the common requirement that a whole floor of an open-plan building be decorated in a consistent pattern so that it will feel "integrated." It begs the question of whether it *should* feel integrated to begin with or should provide more differentiation between groups' areas so that people know when they pass from one to another. To a degree, when a top executive group sets down rules against personalization of group areas, they are also setting rules against effective boundary management by taking choices about the decorative look of a place out of the group's hands.

There is one social factor in subgroup boundary management that is a crucial variable in how effective this process will be. This factor is the group's commitment to creating special events just for themselves (staff meetings, special conferences, periodic communication meetings, and so on) and their commitment to carrying through with these plans under the pressure of conflicting demands from other groups. Simple issues, such as whether to take phone calls while having such an event, are contributors to boundary management. Can the group members efficiently conduct their business with each other, or are they continually being distracted by contacts from outside, so that continuity and momentum are lost? This is a particularly important issue for many staff groups in organizations since the group's reason for existence is basically to provide services to other parts of the system. I strongly believe, however, that the group has to be able to focus inward periodically in order to plan how to use its resources. This will, in turn, make it better able to provide high-quality service or support to other parts of the organization. A group has to be able to tighten its boundaries in order to build an identity and direction as a group, and then loosen that boundary in order to fulfill the mission and move in that direction. There are, of course, ways in which physical features can help this process. The most effective one is probably to hold a meeting off site, out of the organization's spaces altogether, and not accepting phone calls during the meeting.[1]

RELATIONS BETWEEN HEADQUARTERS AND FIELD GROUPS

The interactions between headquarters groups and field units who are physically separated or scattered form a special type of intraorganization boundary relation. So much energy and tension is generated by these relations that they tend to be strained at best. They are subject to stereotyping on both sides, with each group referring to "them" as an entirely alien species, nothing like "us." Information is shared only when it suits someone's hidden purpose, and disclosure of unpleasant facts is minimal if it happens at all. Field groups usually feel that they are the real doers who are keeping things going in spite of the headquarters groups who simply want to constrain and evaluate what they are doing. Headquarters groups feel that field people lack control, responsibility, and a sense of

---

[1]For a fuller discussion of the effects of on-site and off-site meetings, see "The Scene of the Crime," in F. Steele, *Consulting for Organizational Change* (Amherst, Mass.: University of Massachusetts Press, 1975).

the whole, and if left to their own devices, will run the organization into the ground.

In fact, each of these views has some basis, not because of the kinds of people who are in headquarters or field groups, but because the functions of the various groups are bound to be different. But this difference is amplified and distorted by poor boundary management into a gulf where necessary interchanges occur at considerable cost (or not at all). As a result, the whole organization suffers.

Let us consider here some of the ecological aspects of headquarters-field relationships — how the physical setting creates problems in this area and how it can be used as a contributor to improved boundary relations. The first point is the most obvious one: physical separation often leads to little contact, which in turn allows headquarters people to develop untested views of field people, and vice versa. They lack the regular contacts that would generate accurate images of each other. When they do have contacts, they are so fleeting or structured that they tend to tighten the boundary rather than loosen it; for example, field people are being evaluated and headquarters people are the evaluators. Another unfortunate pattern is the tendency, when events are designed for a mix of headquarters and field location people, to hold these events at headquarters most of the time, so that field people feel they are paying all the costs of travel, travel time, and being on someone else's turf. An obvious antidote to this pattern is for those who schedule crossgroup meetings to give careful consideration to varying the location of meetings so that no group feels exploited.

The actual design of headquarters and field locations can be a visible factor affecting intergroup relations, for better or worse. If the look of the headquarters is very different from that of the field locations, it tends to heighten awareness of differences when field people come to visit the headquarters. This is doubly true if the field groups have been held to very tight budget constraints in designing their workplaces, while the headquarters appears (whether true or not) to be designed with an unlimited budget.

Although distance does reduce contact, it occurred to me when working with a client organization that it does not have to mean "out of sight, out of mind." I suggested that the halls at the headquarters building be decorated with pictures of people, places, and things at the field locations. This would serve several purposes, one of which would be to give headquarters people a visual image of people who otherwise would be just voices on the phone or sources of letters through the mail. Another would be to give field people a feeling of connection when they visit the headquarters. They would see pictures of places and people that are familiar. For the organization as a whole, it would serve as an integrating mechanism, a visible demonstration to both residents and visitors, members and nonmembers, that the organization is comprised of many parts, not just what can be seen at headquarters.

There are also instances where effective boundary management calls for an increased separation (tighter boundary) between headquarters and a subunit of the organization. If a regional sales office is located in the headquarters building, it generally has great difficulty in establishing a clear, separate identity with customers until a visibly separate office is established, so that customers are not confused about with whom they are dealing.

Another feature that affects headquarters-field boundary relations is the presence or absence of *places to be* when members of one group are in the other's territory. Are there workplaces in headquarters that have been designated as available to people from field locations, or do they have to always float around or be in someone else's workplace when they are there? Similarly, do headquarters people have areas they can use when they visit a field location? As an external consultant I am well aware of how tiring it is not to have any spot that you can legitimately use on your own, even if it is only to sit and collect your thoughts for a few minutes between meetings. When groups think about the needs of their regular visitors and take the trouble to plan for them, it is both a concrete and symbolic act: it creates better experiences for visitors, which makes it more likely that they will come back, and it communicates thoughtfulness and a desire for a permeable rather than a closed boundary. Having places only for "insider" members sends the opposite message — your placelessness is not our problem.

Headquarters-field relations are also heavily shaped by the electronic communications technology that has been set up to link the two together, or to link all locations into a network. Some obvious examples are good telephone hookups (such as having internal lines that connect distant locations), Telex and Telecopier systems, and the like. One of the most interesting recent developments in this area is that of teleconference technology: the ability for people in widely separated locations to meet via a video-audio hookup so that they can hear and see one another. Similar networks now exist for computer teleconferences. This is still a relatively expensive capability for most organizations, but as the costs come down they will fall below the cumulative time and money costs associated with all the travel that organizational members now do between headquarters and field locations or from one field location to another. It seems obvious that teleconference technology will become widely used and that it will serve to reduce the natural boundaries caused by long distance geographic separation and to increase the ability of members of an organization to hold relatively spontaneous events that are free of the usual logistical headaches associated with getting everybody to one spot at the same time.

RELATIONS BETWEEN THE ORGANIZATION AND ITS ENVIRONMENT

When it comes to physical settings and boundary relations between the organization as a whole and its environment (all the institutions, groups, and individuals that are not part of the organization but that relate to it somehow), many of the same points made above naturally hold true here as well. Physical separation cuts down contact and tightens the boundary, as when an organization's leaders place its facilities in a relatively inaccessible industrial park versus the center of an easily reached city. Even this example has complicating factors: the city location may be easy for *people* to reach but difficult for large trucks, so there are both positive and negative effects of being at a separate site.

The design and decoration of a system's facility will usually have a big effect on its relations with the immediately adjacent community. It may look inviting, have signs telling people that visiting is permitted and showing how to enter, and use glass walls so that some activities in the building are visible to outsiders. On the other hand, it may be built as a relatively impenetrable fortress, showing nothing about activities to the surrounding community and providing no information about whether it is permissible to visit or how to do this. Neither of these is necessarily the better arrangement, since this depends on the type of relationship that the organization's leaders want to have with the community. In some urban areas this has become an adversary relationship, with security being the main concern of both the organization's members and its leaders. Minimizing the number of access points and controlling them well becomes almost an end in itself, with few thoughts about the long-term costs (resentment, lack of community support for company development, and so on) of such a tight boundary between the organization and the community.

SUMMARY

This chapter has focused on two main points. One is that boundary management should be a conscious, focused activity of organizational leaders at all levels of the system. Relations between subunits, or between the system and the various parts of its environment, are heavily affected by the nature of boundaries between them. The quality of these relations in turn affects the health of the system and its parts. The second theme is that there are many ways in which the physical setting sets the pattern for boundaries and influences how well they can be managed, by affecting formal and informal contacts, sending symbolic messages, and so on. An effective manager should always be aware of boundary-related choices he or she is making when designing facilities. This awareness should consider the impact on both resident members who will be using a setting and visitors who will show up there from time to time.

Boundary management can include many subsidiary issues. Designing visible messages at transition zones where groups' areas come together (and possibly overlap) is a particularly sensitive area. Key choices to be made include how much to emphasize sharp differentiation or a gradual transition, how to treat style differences or similarities, and whether to promote free access or controlled movement between the groups. The prime need is to develop a model of desired boundary relations that allows managers to know whether a particular boundary between their group and another should be tight or loose, as well as when this should be modified because of changed needs or work patterns. Both loosening or tightening boundaries can make sense when based on an underlying concept of systemic needs. Conversely, each can be arbitrary and unrelated to effectiveness when it occurs because of personal whims or traditional standards that continually get applied without conscious attention to the boundary management issue.

CHAPTER 14

Settings, Organizational Climate, and the Quality of Work Life

The final organizational ecology dimension we will consider is one of the most fundamental, at least from the standpoint of what members of an organization experience as they work day-to-day. It is the impact of settings on organization climate and quality of work life. These have become greater concerns in the past five years or so, as there has been an upsurge in awareness of the costs over time to both individuals and organizations of a debilitating organizational climate or poor experiences at work that tend to degrade and depress workers. Unions have emphasized this as an example of the unsatisfied needs of members, and many managers of human resource functions have cited this as an impetus for upgrading both the basic facilities for workers and the opportunities to affect their own work lives in more meaningful ways than in the past. What I am concerned with here is an amalgamation of all the previously discussed ecological effects, literally the "feel of the workplace" as a sociophysical setting for daily work life. Although organizational climate and experienced quality of work life are closely related, I will treat them separately.

SETTINGS AND ORGANIZATIONAL CLIMATE

It is obvious that an organization's physical settings contribute a great deal to its climate — in fact, some people think of only the physical side when the term organizational climate is used. However, physical climate is clearly only one part of the total "feel" of a workplace for members. Management patterns, operating policies, central myths of the organization, and social norms also help to provide the total feel for members.

When I have looked at organizational climate in my work, I have

146

tended to assess it in terms of its impact on members and on the feel of the system as a whole, much as one would describe the impact of the weather in different geographic regions.[1] This metaphor leads to four basic indicators of climate in an organization:

1. *Amount of energy.*   Is the climate a brisk one that stirs people to action and tends to make events happen, or is it an enervating one that reduces the levels of energy and excitement for individuals and groups?
2. *Distribution of energy.*   Whether the total human energy is high or low, there is also the question of how it gets distributed or used. Does it go into actions aimed at goal attainment or system development, or does it mainly go into maintenance-oriented or self-protective behaviors (like having to wear a tiresome heavy overcoat all the time in a very cold climate)?
3. *Amount of pleasure.*   Climates also vary in terms of how much pleasure they provide for people who live in them. In terms of both weather and social climate this is a subjective issue, since the perfect climate for one person may be objectionable to another person. One indicator of the pleasure dimension in an organization is simply the extent to which people seem to be happy and alive when there rather than glum and despondent.
4. *Potential for growth.*   To what extent is the climate one that stimulates people to develop new skills, abilities, knowledge, and understanding so that they grow in competence? Some organizations seem to place a lot of emphasis on development as a key task of management, while others give it very little conscious attention.

With this introduction, let us now consider further the impact of workplace settings on each climate dimension.

Amount of Energy

Since this area has already been discussed in Chapter 10, I will not go into detail here. I would simply emphasize that a system's energy level is often the result of a complex (and subtle) interaction process that includes personal energy levels, social/management climate, and the pattern and look of the physical settings in which action takes place.

---

[1]Many of the ideas in this section were first formulated in Fritz Steele and Stephen Jenks, *The Feel of the Workplace* (Reading, Mass.: Addison-Wesley, 1977), ch. 8–9.

Distribution of Energy

After sensing roughly how much human energy there is in an organization, the next issue is to discover what people *do* with that energy: how is it directed or used, and what are the net effects on the organization's ability to survive and be successful? Because this issue has been considered in Chapter 11, I will not repeat the discussion here.

Amount of Pleasure

The impact of settings on the pleasantness of a climate is well known, although not always fully considered when workplaces are being designed. The first point is one made earlier: pleasant climates are by definition at least partly an individual issue. What we can say is that generally people will like a setting more if they have a hand in creating it than if it is totally imposed on them by some outside person or system.

Given this generalization, there are some physical characteristics of workplaces that tend to create higher and lower pleasure climates. Work that produces noxious stimuli — noise, strong smells, glaring light, temperature extremes — requires a setting that compensates for these or a work process that allows people to get away in order to relieve the stress and fatigue caused by the difficult climate. In a more subtle way, settings that are bland or dull to a large percentage of their users tend to be unpleasant over the long haul, even though the users do not feel justified in saying that they are awful. There is nothing technically wrong with them, yet they force many people to tune themselves out all day long in order not to feel discouraged or depressed by their workplace. This is a waste of human experience potential, since it generally costs little more to make a workplace visually interesting than it does to make it dull.

Organizational climate is also influenced on the pleasure dimension by the physical location of the facility. Nice views, interesting neighborhoods and shops, lively urban surroundings, easily reached recreational facilities, and generally good weather for using such facilities — all contribute to people's enjoyment of organizational membership. It is becoming more recognized that where a system is located is an aspect of its climate just as much as structure and management processes are. On the average, people are more likely these days to expect more from the climate in which they work, both socially and physically, so that organizational leaders need to consider this as a factor in obtaining and retaining competent members who will be excited about contributing to the organization. My hope is that managers will consider members' pleasure as a relevant climate variable, rather than as something unrelated or even in conflict with "getting the job done." There is no reason why the job cannot be done in a workplace people like; in fact, they are more likely to be there getting the job done if the whole setting is a pleasurable one for them.

Potential for Growth

In most work organizations, managers tend to be unaware of the potential of the work setting as a stimulator of growth for users, but it can be just that if it is designed right. One of the key characteristics of a high-growth setting is that it offers opportunities for people to make changes, try things out, and learn about the effects of what they did. Conversely, settings where everything is fixed (either by design or by rules about not tinkering with anything) tend to contribute little to growth in users' awareness or competence.

The location of facilities is another growth factor. People can be located within an organization's spaces in spots where they see a lot of the events of the system and come in contact with a variety of types of people, or they can be located in isolated spots where they seldom encounter anyone except the members of their immediate work group. The former spot will, on the average, be a greater contributor to developing members' maturity and awareness of differences.

Sometimes the locational issue is closely tied to a particular management style and structure. For instance, in a sales-oriented company, a particular level of supervisors tended to complain that the people who reported to them were not of high caliber and did not have the potential to develop judgment, initiative, and risk-taking skills. They suggested more stringent hiring criteria be developed to get a better class of telephone sales and trouble-shooting people. In analyzing the situation, it emerged that the supervisors' desks were usually adjacent or very near to the sales persons' desks and well within earshot. The supervisors had a regular pattern of second-guessing and short-circuiting the actions and judgments of their subordinates; they would overhear telephone conversations and motion to the subordinates to change their answers, or they would pick up the phone and take over the calls themselves.

It was suggested as an experiment that the supervisors' desks be moved to a less "handy" area where they would not have minute-to-minute contact with their charges. As a result, the sales people were allowed to use their own judgments (very reluctantly at first). Some of their decisions worked and some of them did not, but many of the people began to be seen as more competent and having potential. The physical setting had been allowing a pattern of dominance that looked like it was simply a failing on the part of the subordinates, not an artifact of the management style of the supervisors. From the standpoint of improving the growth climate in this unit, the best move was to physically make it hard for the supervisors to continue that style, since the long-run cost of blocking development was more than the cost of occasional mistakes as the subordinates made more of their own decisions.

Finally, a workplace may be a stimulator of growth for a whole group if they are charged with the responsibility of shaping it and managing it as one of their tools for getting results. Conversely, when these decisions are controlled outside the group, the members do not have this medium available as a challenge to doing things better and learning how better to work with each other, resolve conflicts, and set mutual goals that benefit all members.

IMPACT OF WORKPLACES ON QUALITY OF WORK LIFE

In turning to the issue of the impact of the workplace on members' quality of work life (QWL), we get into an even fuzzier area than with organizational climate. QWL has been a hot term for several years, and it has often been used as one of the focuses for improving American work organizations. I think the operative term should actually be "experienced quality of work life," since it is people's experiences on the job that determine whether they feel productive, fulfilled, and satisfied. An outside observer may judge the quality of a person's work situation to be low, but the real question is how the person experiences it.

It is obvious that the physical workplace will play a part in determining whether people feel that they have high-quality experiences on the job.[2] At the simplest level, having good spaces, high-quality furnishings, and necessary technical supports, such as efficient telephone, copying, and mail systems, all help create a sense of quality in one's environment. The same goes for decorative elements, especially if there is a design philosophy that has been influential in the choices of colors, materials, art works, graphics, and the like. Organizations where all these choices get made in a slipshod or backhanded manner tend to have settings that do not seem of high quality to their users. My assumption is that over the long term these settings have a negative impact on users' feelings about

---

[2]This section is based in part on my chapter, "Humanizing the Physical Setting at Work," in H. Meltzer and F. Wickert (eds.), *Humanizing Organizational Behavior* (Springfield, Ill.: Charles C. Thomas Publishers, 1976).

themselves as well. Since people in most organizations spend half or more of their waking hours at work, this effect can be considerable over time, which is why there is the growing concern over people's experienced quality of work life. In addition, I would suggest that a poor, thoughtlessly planned physical setting tends to make workers feel *out of place*, that is, they cope with the low quality by rejecting the setting so that they feel they are in limbo. The alternative is to accept it as one's place and therefore to accept oneself as deserving low-quality, dull, or demeaning surroundings, which is not a very good option either.

In a sense, the preceding discussion of organizational climate was about quality of work life as well, since the organization's climate is a big force in what people experience in their work lives. What was not dealt with, however, was the impact of the organization's characteristic spatial decision processes on experienced quality of work life. I have believed for a long time that the *how* of physical environments (how they were created, how they are managed, how they can be changed or re-evaluated) is as big a factor in people's satisfaction as is the *what* (the actual design and layout of personal and group workplaces).

As we saw in Parts I and II, in those organizations where the "how" factor depresses the quality of work life, there tends to be a consistent pattern of spatial decision making: the top of the organization holds tight control, and most other levels feel relatively powerless to experiment or tamper with the overall design. The emphasis is on integrated design, which usually means that a single design theme preferred by top members is applied across the organization's groups and levels. Middle managers and lower-level workers are expected not to take responsibility for their own settings and are trained not to do so. There is a high expressed concern for maintaining the places and things of the organization, and relatively little attention is paid to what this focus costs in the maintenance of the health of the people in the system. Personalization of workplaces is considered to be vandalism, which suggests that the users are there to support the facilities, not vice versa. The net effect is a reduced quality of work life as perceived by the average member, even if the facilities are luxurious on some objective scale. The experience of having and using the facilities is a constant reminder of one's powerlessness and inconsequentiality.

Efforts to improve experienced quality of work life, then, should include an opening up of the processes of facilities decision making. In many organizations the opposite approach is used, which is to unilaterally create a "better" working environment and move everyone into it. This is usually followed by frustration and surprise that the troops are not universally grateful for all that has been done for them. In many instances a greater improvement in perceived quality of work life would have been achieved with much cheaper solutions if the various levels of the system had been more involved in the decisions that affected their own work areas the most.

SUMMARY

Both organizational climate and experienced quality of work life are heavily influenced by the nature of workplaces — their design, how they got the way they are, and how much freedom and encouragement there is to alter them in order that they continue to be useful and appropriate as users' needs change. The tone for a relatively humanistic process — for aiming for a supportive climate and a high perceived quality of work life — must clearly come first from the organization's top leaders. If they do not value these organizational characteristics very much, neither will those who are below them in the structure, no matter what their private views might be. Their official decisions and actions will reinforce a mechanistic view of facilities as a top-owned resource temporarily shared with lower-power people who should be grateful for whatever they get. What will be missing is the opposite viewpoint, of the organization as an organism that cannot be separated from its social and physical environments and of members whose ecological experiences in their workplaces are influenced by both the nature of those settings and by the processes that are used to create, maintain, and control them.

Part IV

FUTURE APPLICATIONS
IN
WORKPLACE MANAGEMENT

In this final part the concepts and suggestions from the four previous parts are applied to some specific problem areas in organizational design. In Chapter 15 I emphasize the opportunities for new executive team settings (and work styles) because such settings have been the scene of so little innovation and experimentation.

Chapter 16 deals with several other application areas that were chosen because of their high-leverage possibilities (i.e., more conscious design and use will have a particularly high payoff). And Chapter 17 is an articulation of the primary assumptions and design principles that have formed the basis for my point of view in this book.

CHAPTER 15

The Ecology
of Executive Teams

In this chapter I will focus primarily on the possibilities for improving the physical settings in which executive teams operate. I have chosen to focus on the design and use of executive team spaces because this seems to be a neglected area where useful innovations are long overdue. A considerable amount of effort has been expended in recent years in analyzing and improving such workplaces as factories, hospitals, laboratories, and the like, where tasks are relatively well defined and tied closely to physical equipment. A trend is now developing toward conducting work analyses of and redesigning settings for white-collar office and clerical tasks. Such activities have, in a sense, been supported by the top executives in organizations; they are the ones who ask the questions that lead to such studies, and it is they who usually approve the budgets that make them happen. But the focus of these studies has generally been on groups and levels of the organization other than the top executive. There has been, to my knowledge, much less attention paid to the ways in which executive groups do their work and the spatial implications of such patterns.

My basic contention here is that stereotyped expectations about executive team "work" lead to stereotyped settings chosen mainly for symbolic reasons, on the basis of (1) commonly held images of what an "executive area" ought to look like to impress visitors, (2) what the members are entitled to because of their senior ranks in the hierarchy, and (3) their personal preferences, reflecting their images of self-importance. What tends to receive much less consideration is the question of systemic impact: in what ways does the setting influence the executive team's functioning and the functioning of the system as a whole? This pattern represents a perfect example of the circular influence process in human ecology; stereotypical notions about executive groups and their "needs" lead to stereotypical physical settings, which in turn tend to shape executive team members' actions into relatively narrow and predictable channels that may be adequate much of the time, but that are constraining when new viewpoints or solutions are needed for new problems. This suggests, then, that there is an untapped potential here, with scope for real organization development if we can clearly sort out how those in an executive team do their work, how they could work if they were more flexible, and how the setting should be arranged to broaden their range of options. To this end, we will examine the nature of executive teams, the nature of their work, typical physical settings for executive groups (and the problems they cause), and a set of implications for change in both the work of the group and the design of their work settings.

CHARACTERISTICS AND ACTIVITIES
OF EXECUTIVE TEAMS

What are "executive teams"? For our purposes here, this term applies to the top two levels of management in a company (often the president and the people who report to the president) *if* they tend to work together at least part of the time as a team instead of working independently on their separate, differentiated responsibilities. Obviously, not all groups of executives would fit into this definition of executive teams, but many do.

The prime characteristics of an executive team would include the following:

- The executives play two roles — (1) as the head of a specific, differentiated part or function, and (2) as an executive of the whole.
- Their reward system is structured to reward high performance in both roles, not just that as head of an individual function.
- The executives are curious and concerned about events throughout the system, not just those in their own area of responsibility. It is considered all right and valuable for team members to show concern for and to help one another, or to show displeasure with and challenge one another.
- There is a multiple interaction pattern among the executives, not just a series of one-to-ones between the leader and each executive.
- As a team they influence policies, mission, directions, and patterns, not just single events or short-term products.

- The team members tend to spend their time and energy on several kinds of agenda: managing existing activities; gathering information, synthesizing it, and predicting future trends; managing or influencing future events and development patterns in the organization; and managing and developing others to carry out the first two.
- One of the team's major responsibilities (although one that is overlooked by many groups of executives) is to create effective feedback processes among themselves, between themselves and the rest of the organization, and between the organization and its environment.

In summary, the true executive team is a group of executives who concern themselves with the health of two entities: their own areas of responsibility and the overall organization. These concerns tend to cluster in a number of areas: definition of missions and establishment of goals; relations with the environment (or with other units, if the focus is a unit of the organization); division and integration of work; the generation of and access to valid information about what is happening in the organization and the surrounding environment; processes for problem finding, problem solving, and decision making; the stimulation and effective direction of human energy; processes of individual and organizational learning and renewal; and design, alteration, and management of physical systems.

Although there is not necessarily a single model of how executive teams should operate to meet the above criteria and concerns, a number of obvious activities are the backbone of an executive team's process. With pretty fair certainty we can say that the executives will be doing some or all of the following activities in their workplace:

- Sitting and thinking, standing and thinking, or walking and thinking
- Writing (notes, papers, memos, and so on)
- Reading (notes, letters, magazines, reports, and so on)
- Talking to each other and to people who are not members of the team
- Taking part in meetings (among themselves, as a whole team, or with nonteam people)
- Eating, using washroom facilities, and possibly sleeping
- Seeking information (from one another, from their organizational members, from outsiders, from such impersonal sources as files, libraries, electronic mass media, and so forth)
- Planning events or actions (for themselves, for subunits, or for the organization as a whole)
- Getting around and observing what is going on in areas other than those in the vicinity of their own personal workplaces

- Attempting to influence one another or other people
- Trying to stimulate action if things do not seem to be happening
- Collecting information to test the quality of decisions and the accuracy of predictions about the future
- Observing, testing, stimulating, directing, and managing human energy in the organization
- Expressing their own style, needs, preferences, interests, and so forth through the ways they control and influence their own immediate settings.

This is a very full list of possible activities for any one person, yet the day-to-day experiences of many executives tend to become relatively narrow because they are constrained into habit patterns that do not seem to develop the potential of such activities. This is partly because most executive teams fail to recognize that they are truly a team, an organism with patterned relationships that can take many forms, not just engage in the "normal" workday routines.

EXECUTIVE ROW OFFICE SETTINGS

The habit patterns of executive teams get reflected in the physical layouts and social norms that serve as controls on team interaction. For instance, a typical executive area arrangement is shown in Figure 15.1. The president is in the highest-status office, which is the one in the corner with two window walls, and the executives (E_1, E_2, and so forth) who report to the president are strung out along the two corridors. (S stands for secretarial work stations.) In addition, there are usually several meeting rooms. The decorations in the executive area tend to be tastefully done and to symbolically represent a greater investment than those in comparable areas in other parts of the building. Furniture is usually of higher quality than elsewhere in the organization, and the whole area tends to be decorated in an integrated fashion that reflects one person's taste and choices.

In such an area, individuals sit in their private offices at their desks, meet in a conference room, or talk in small groups (two to four or five people) in offices. The executives tend to send for lower-level managers to come to meetings with them, rather than going out to meet people. There is usually no common or communal area other than the conference room, and, therefore, the executives tend to have little informal, non-planned contact with each other or other organization members. There is also relatively low visibility; because people normally cannot see each

Figure 15.1
A Typical "Executive Row" Layout

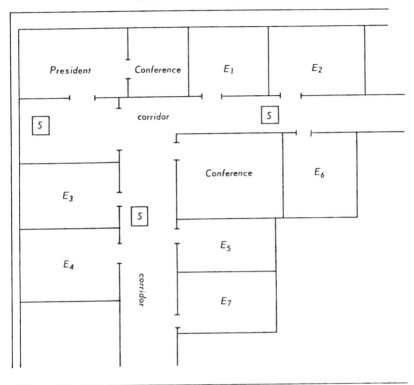

other, it is hard to have a sense of what is happening there — especially if you are a visitor passing through. The executive area itself is frequently located on the highest floor of the building (representing status, presumably) and therefore tends to discourage people from "passing through" anyway.

In an alternative executive group layout, "the dispersion model," the president and a small personal staff are located somewhere, but the executives who report to the president are located wherever their functional groups are located. There is no executive row as such. In this case the individual executives frequently re-create the executive row layout in their own areas, installing themselves in the spot labeled "president" in Figure 15.1.

Impact on Executive Team Functioning

The effects of an executive row layout will, of course, depend on a number of factors, including the climate and norms of the executive group, the president's leadership style, the executive group's effectiveness at identifying tasks and managing their own processes, and the nature of the business in which their organization is engaged. Other things being equal, however, certain effects tend to result from the standard layout just described. For one, the executives tend not to see the workings of other people and parts of the system in a natural manner. Either they see people who are venturing into "executive turf" and are therefore usually self-conscious, or when they do go somewhere else in the system for a meeting, they tend to get treated as if they were making an inspection tour. The experience is orchestrated by managers who want to shape the impressions that the executive forms about an area.

To the extent that the executive area is tastefully designed as a whole, individual executives tend to feel less ownership and identification with their own spots. As an executive once said to me, "Don't pay any attention to this office. It reflects the position as it is supposed to be, not me as I am." The result can be a group of people who feel relatively transient, as if they were visitors temporarily occupying plush quarters but with no claim on any personal traces there. Other staff members also tend to get very little sense of the executives as people during their visits to executive row offices.

Lack of Communal Space

The lack of any communal spaces or central gathering spots in the executive row layout leads to a relatively stereotyped pattern of interactions, without much spontaneity or spur-of-the-moment crossfertilization of ideas. The area at the turn of the corridor (refer to Figure 15.1) might be used for this, but not in a vital, encouraging way — and such activity would probably be discouraged by the president's secretary who has to get work done while sitting in the middle of that space. Other than that location, the layout has no real "center," no core where stimulating interactions would tend to happen. People would therefore tend to spend most of their time in their own private offices unless they had some specific event to attend. This, in turn, reinforces the tendency to concentrate on one's own area of responsibility, rather than visualizing all areas of responsibility in relation to one other and to the whole as an organic entity of its own. The spatial layout almost directs the executives (and those who interact with them) to compartmentalize each area of responsibility.

From the standpoint of the executive team as the corporation leadership, there is a stronger pattern of secrecy and privacy than their roles warrant and than staff members, stockholders, and the board of directors should expect or demand. Although they are not elected officials, the executives' power to affect the welfare of members and the organization as a whole suggests that their style and actions should be relatively visible to set a tone for the system as well as to be open to scrutiny and second guessing (which may not make leaders feel comfortable but does tend to keep them reality-centered). The tone set by the typical executive row layout and remote location tends to be the opposite. Low disclosure is the pattern; "We'll tell you what we think you need to know" is the command; "We'll send for you when we want to interact" is the rule of working; and "Keep it hidden if it might cause us problems" is the internal norm that executive group members enforce on one another. The layout sends all these messages to the rest of the organization, as well as making it easier for the executives to adhere to these behaviors.

Strong Emphasis on Status Symbols

Using status to determine location and size of offices costs an executive team a good bit of flexibility, because once the area is tailor-made to fit positions, the cost of shifting people around becomes considerable, especially if you have to maintain the same relative differentials in status symbols. To be most helpful, the physical configuration of the executive team should change over time with changing demands or special assignments for subgroups of the executive team, but this would cause confusion in the status symbol language so it tends not to happen. (It also fails to happen because of a built-in inertia, so that once places get set up they tend to stay that way — much like people taking the same seats around the meeting table each week.) One of the costs is that the executives' fixed locations make it less likely that they will interact in new ways or look at problems in different lights; one must sometimes get out of a habitual setting to perceive new patterns or issues.

Difficulty of Communication

The existence of an executive row and the lack of a central gathering place that would attract people from different areas and levels of the organization lead to a tendency for the executive team to be slow in forming a picture of what is happening elsewhere in the organization. There are no gathering points where such information naturally comes together and no place for the executives to informally talk and exchange information on trends or issues to which they should pay more attention.

This is made even more difficult by the typical lack of graphic displays of data about current performance or trends in the quantitative measures used to track the course of the organization's activities. These data have a very different impact when they are posted on a wall than when they are filed away in reports lodged in the drawers of each individual's office desk. A visible display tends to promote comment whenever two or more people are looking at it. When the data are in a report, they usually get discussed only when they are an agenda topic at a planned meeting — a much skimpier treatment that lacks potential for real discovery of hidden trends.

Summary of Problems

A number of typical problems arise from the ways in which the top executive groups in U.S. companies tend to be structured physically and socially. For one, executives tend to play stereotyped roles with relatively little experimentation in renegotiating role expectations — either with the head of the group or with the layer of management directly below them. Second, the interactions among the executive group members tend to be patterned by habit and precedent, with little experimentation with more spontaneous, informal interactions. Third, because of both role expectations and interactional norms, the executives tend to be limited in what they can do as individuals and as a team, especially in the area of spotting, defining, and solving emerging human-system problems that have not had a tradition of getting regular attention from top management; "discovery" is a hard process for them.

Fourth, executives tend to be constricted in their options about physical layout, relative locations, choices of furniture and decorations, and degree of personalization of the whole area because they feel obliged to set a good example for "maintaining standards" (that is, keeping people in their places) throughout the organization. However, they seldom articulate what this rigidity costs them in terms of constraining the ways in which they can do their work. Fifth, there tends to be little value placed on innovation in the ways in which the executive team does its work, even though the organization itself may have technological or marketing innovation as one of its prime goals. There is a natural conservative force on the executives' style of doing their work, and it tends to carry over to how they shape their work space. Their norms tend to enforce conformity in their dealings with one another, as well as in the public face that they show to the rest of the company and the outside world.

Lastly, when the executives function as a group of separate individuals relating to the president one-on-one or dealing with each other on issues that relate directly to their own functional areas (a pattern that is reinforced by a row of separate offices or spaces for them to file themselves away in), there will be little identification with the whole, little sense of team action that everyone owns, a tendency for functional responsibilities to always drive out the executive-of-the-whole point of view, frequent battles over jurisdiction and ways of measuring individual performance (with almost no attention or energy put into specifically measuring executive group performance), and tight boundaries maintained between the units. Integration tends to be treated as the top person's problem — "Harry will do it if Harry wants it done." In other words, the general pattern is for the top management to be an executive *group* because employees perceive them to be a collectivity, but not much of an executive *team* because they do not meet the criteria listed earlier.

SUPPORTIVE SETTINGS FOR EXECUTIVE TEAMS

Having pinpointed the problems attributed to executive row office settings, here I want to provide some concrete recommendations about how an organizational ecology point of view can contribute to the development of an effective executive team through making the physical setting and norms about its use as supportive as possible.

I should begin by stating clearly that I do not believe that there is one single "right" way for an executive team to structure its workspaces. Different players, styles, and periods in the company's development call for different strengths from the company's leadership, so presumably the setting should be somewhat different as well. The point is that an ecological point of view is needed to be aware of the ways in which the layout and the group's norms shape the activities, work patterns, and experiences of the team members, as well as their relationships to the rest of the organization.

Based on the list of common tasks presented earlier, a supportive setting for executive team action should have a number of characteristics. It should provide good places for working alone, working in pairs, working in groups of more than two, and interacting informally — not necessarily on something labeled "work." These events could be both planned and spontaneous.

A supportive setting should provide appropriate access to and from other members of the organization, so that the executives are not walled off from each other. It should similarly provide good connections with the outside world, for information gathering, storage, retrieval, display, and so forth.

It should heighten executives' awareness of their responsibility to promote both the interests of their own units and the mission, values, and goals of the organization as a whole. It should be consistent with the values, norms, climate, goals, and sense of identity that the executive team is trying to promote in the organization.

A supportive setting should allow room for experimentation and innovation in the ways people do their work, without the necessity for big decisions and major costs. And finally, the workplace should provide an enjoyable setting for team members so that they like spending time there.

Although there is no single design that fulfills all these criteria, there are certain kinds of features that, on the average, provide a high-quality environment for an executive team. These will be considered in the sections that follow.

Tone of the Workplace

The executive team should keep in mind that their immediate workplace sets the tone for the rest of the organization, whether or not that is their intention. One element of this tone is design related, namely, the style of layout and furnishings (for example, the decisions between open versus closed layouts, central spaces versus a linear layout, or traditional office furniture versus various alternative styles). If the executives choose a decorative style that is totally different from that of the rest of the organization's workspaces, there is a clear tradeoff: it may enhance their image, but it increases the social gap between them and the rest of the staff thus making it harder to stay in touch with internal organizational realities.

In general, executives should choose the look or tone they want to set with the idea in mind that they are all affected by it, as a personal workplace and as a result of the messages relayed to the rest of the organization. In many organizations this tone is set by the top executive or a delegated decision maker, neither of whom generally consult very much with the other executive team members. In such situations, the other executives have to live with the consequences of a design that was not openly explored or discussed by them as a team.

The second aspect of the organizational tone set by executives relates to their use of their workplace. Members of the system's other levels will tend to be more aware of workplace management issues and how to approach them if the executive team visibly influences its own ecological experience by openly conducting periodic evaluations of their setting, diagnosing problems, considering options, making changes in design, and altering social norms and use policies to suit changing needs. Conversely, an executive team that seems to ignore these processes sends a message to the rest of the system about how little they value other groups' abilities to do this well.

Location in the System

Another tricky question, to which there is definitely no single right answer, is where to physically place executives in the facility. Whether the executive team should be placed together or dispersed among their own units depends on power relationships, the kinds of teamwork they want to engage in, the history of executives' impacts on the system, and the degree of independence or subservice that the executives want to promote among those who report directly to them. If it is logistically possible, I recommend a "linked-dispersion" model where the president and executives are relatively close to one another in a sort of wheel arrangement, and each individual executive is also near those who report directly to him or her. A typical rectangle floor plan obviously does not lend itself very well to such a layout. A circular building tends to be much better, but office buildings are almost never built in a circular or oval plan, so the linked-dispersion model is usually hard to work out.

When it is impossible to implement a linked-dispersion model, I opt for the "two-seat" model, in which the executives have two workplaces— one in the executive area and one in the middle of their own function or group. Such an arrangement is frequently viewed as a waste of space, especially if one of the offices does not get used, which will happen if the executives do not work as a team. Executives need to set a norm about making conscious choices about where to be, so they do not fall into a habit pattern of just rooting themselves in one place or the other. The dual office approach is also a less wasteful design if the offices are relatively modest in size, so that the combined size of the two does not use much more floor area than one grand executive office. The executives can make this work or block it, of course, depending on how willing they are to let go of the traditional image of what they have a "right" to expect in an office. They have to feel that the expanded effectiveness that comes from two good functional locations is worth giving up the single high-symbolic spot.

COMMUNAL AREAS

In terms of the ways in which the executive team members interact with one another, most executive area layouts tend to minimize necessary interactions and keep the team from developing greater competence at teamwork. Most executive teams that want to function as a true team, with high disclosure and high mutual influence, could benefit from a well-executed open-plan layout in which they are visible to one another. Yet most executives cannot make the necessary conceptual and emotional shift from their image of what a person of their importance deserves as a workplace to accept an open-plan layout. The question is, then, what other strategies can be used to promote effective interaction among the executives?

For some groups, including in the design a central open lounge area with good seating, coffee or food, and so forth could work. Another kind of "magnet" facility would be a central information room with graphic displays of current operating data, television, Telex, and other hookups to other locations and the outside world. This would serve as a kind of "war room" where people could gather information and talk about trends on the spot, rather than waiting for some scheduled future meeting in which trends would be on the agenda. Using the same place for gathering information, making it visible, and talking about it increases the likelihood that the executives will spot trends and emerging problems as a team (as opposed to letting whoever on the team happens to be good at this do so). This approach promotes a way of working that is more "additive" than usual — that is, people can quickly build upon, challenge, or influence one another's ideas.

A way of freeing up space for communal areas is to cut down on the size of private spaces so that they serve just their intended purpose — a place to withdraw and be secluded. That requires a relatively small spot (or "cave"), as long as there are a variety of sizes of meeting spaces (or "courts") available for interactive tasks. One layout that combines these features would look like a town center or an elegant French farmyard, with executives' private spaces ringed around a central commons area and various other meeting spaces located adjacent to the central space (see Figure 15.2). Alternatively, each executive might have a traditional size (that is, large) space that is open to the views of others and visitors, but there would also be a sliding screen (in the Japanese mode) that could be drawn across the end that is nearest to other people when he or she wanted to be in a very private mode. If the executives really used this flexibility and changed the screen positions with changing mood or needs, the whole area would have a fascinating vitality to it, because its look or feel at any given time would depend on the particular pattern of open and closed screens.

Accessibility to the Organization

There is the fundamental question of how accessible the executives feel they should be — as individuals and as a team — to fulfill their dual roles as heads of areas and executives of the whole. If an executive group

Figure 15.2
ONE POSSIBLE LAYOUT FOR PROMOTING RICHER EXECUTIVE-TEAM INTERACTION

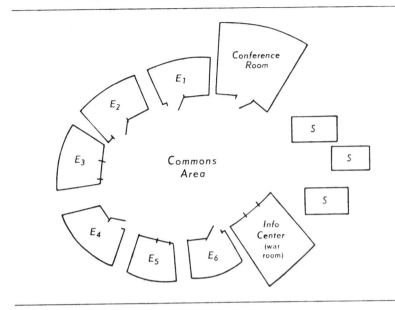

wants to maintain a great social distance, then the typical executive floor location (top of the building, not on the way to anywhere, separate from all other functional areas) and layout (lineup of private offices, challenging secretaries, no community space) are probably right for them. If they want to reduce the gap, some things can be done. One is not to decorate the executive offices on a much higher standard than the other areas of the building; the less difference, the less people will be reminded to be nervous when they step into the area (and the less others will resent the way their own design needs are taken care of).

Another approach is to think seriously about the executive area's *location*. Placing it in a more central location so that people pass through it on the way to other places takes a lot of the mystery out of the territory. It also creates a center of activity that will help executives stay in touch with the staff's moods, rather than being filed away in a backwater that never gets spontaneous news. Having an executive area in a central location also allows more people to see top leaders coming and going (and vice versa), which in turn creates a greater ease in dealing with each other, unless the executives use the visibility to "check up" on people's movements. Then increased visibility will probably increase the social distance between the top levels and the rest of the system.

Accessibility can also be fostered by the ways in which the executives use space. They can obviously reduce the gap by choosing not to hold all meetings or events in their own offices or conference rooms. They can easily break this usual pattern by sometimes going to other people's areas. The executives would probably have to initiate this because there is usually an organizational norm that says that a person should always defer to a higher-ranking executive in terms of decisions about place.

As soon as possible, after a new executive area is opened, the occupants should schedule events that draw others there on a regular basis, to familiarize them with the setting and make it legitimate to enter. Having some sort of shared facility, such as a lounge, would also accomplish this; many executives, however, would not use such a facility if subordinates also used it regularly.

Promoting Experimentation

If a leadership group is trying to promote a greater sense of innovation and experimentation in their organization, they need to be consistent by demonstrating an innovative spirit in the way in which they do their own work and where they do it. Instituting the "war room" concept would send a message to others about the value of trying to cut down lag time in getting information and spotting trends. Building in changeability (and using it) in their own area sends a different message than creating a rock-hard permanent monument to the group's importance.

Experimenting with new kinds of events and new locations for events tends to break down old norms about the right or acceptable ways that things can happen. Being willing to ease some of their own needs for status symbols can help loosen the grip that the symbolic language holds on managers' abilities to rearrange people's offices according to task and interaction criteria rather than just by who deserves which class of available office space.

Finally, one of the clearest signals from the top about innovation is for the executive group to create a process for getting feedback from other staff members about the impact of the executive layouts and climate on them — in terms of access, feel, functionality, and the like. The point is to make it easy for the staff members to share their opinions, and easy for the executives to hear them.

SUMMARY

In this chapter my intent has been to focus on executive team ecology as a microcosm of the ecology of the organization as a whole. To be an effective team over a period of time, any executive group should deal consciously with questions such as: What is the nature of our work, as individuals and as a group? Are we stuck in habit patterns that should be changed to help us innovate our own work styles? How does our physical setting affect us and the rest of the members of our organization? Are there ways in which we could change traditional executive area designs to promote better interaction, team awareness, accessibility, and connection with the outside world? Can we deal with these questions in a relatively open manner that will also stimulate a spirit of inquiry and innovation in other parts of the organization?

Many executive groups would not be interested in or see the value in asking themselves such questions, but I think they will interest those top leadership groups that aspire to perform as true executive teams.

CHAPTER 16

High–Leverage
Ecological Applications

This chapter will look at four high-potential applications of the organizational ecology approach to today's office situations. The first three deal with designing and managing workplaces for task forces and temporary teams; for training, learning, and developmental activities; and for offices that incorporate new technologies. In the last section I want to consider the process of social engineering to change habitual-use patterns when making physical-settings changes.

SPECIAL TREATMENT FOR TASK FORCES OR TEMPORARY TEAMS

Work organizations are constantly creating groups of people who are defined as a team for doing some particular task, with the expectation of a defined, finite life to the group and the dispersal of the members into other groups or positions when the tasks of the temporary team have been completed. These temporary teams vary tremendously in effectiveness, some doing excellent work and others being never quite able to get themselves together as a team, let alone to produce quality work. Many factors would contribute to the success or failure of the temporary team, of course. One of the factors that cuts across all situations is the *ecology* of the team: how it is shaped physically and how its settings are managed and used. This is the area that will be examined here.

Typical Issues

There are a number of fairly predictable problems or issues that tend to be present in the working of a temporary team inside an organization. One may derive from the way the team was created if team members were selected at random with little prior consultation about whether they want to be on it or consideration about whether that mix of individuals can work together.

170

A second problem is treating the change as only a paper one, and leaving everyone's workplaces where they are on the assumption that the team's physical existence will simply be through coming together for meetings (which ignores the value of all the nonmeeting team contacts that can build a strong sense of team identity). If the team does get assigned a workplace of its own, this place is often chosen by what space is vacant, not by specific criteria about size, nature, and location required for the team to work effectively. Groups that are defined on the "real" organization chart tend to be treated as higher priority than a temporary team, no matter what the potential payoff from the temporary team's doing a good job. This also implies that a temporary team gets treated as a sort of nonentity: since it is planned to have a finite life, it is almost as if it did not really exist at all, even though very few of the formal "permanent" groups actually go on forever. The transiency is just more obvious when it is defined as one of the team's characteristics.

Another common pattern is that a temporary group often tries to "hit the ground running." They start their existence together by immediately working on the content of their task. This stems at least in part from anxiousness about time constraints and being a temporary grouping, but it neglects the necessary start-up work that is required to build an effective temporary group: clarifying mission and goals, setting norms about how members will work, defining likely working problems and how they will be handled, clarifying leadership and other influence processes, and generally setting expectations about how members will relate to each other and to the other parts of the organization. One key ecological area of expectations is the pattern of members' contacts: when, how, and where they will work together, and what they are expected to do when working individually. Identifying these issues and patterns early would help a temporary team consciously shape members' experiences with one another, but this step tends to be skipped more often than not.

By remaining in their old offices, getting together just for meetings, and jumping into task content before building an effective process, the group never becomes a team, since the members lack a critical mass of experiences with one another. Their potential is not realized in their performance: some groups do a mediocre job; others are not able to get the job done at all.

Effective Approaches

There are a number of physical design aspects that I have found to be useful in facilitating the effective development and working of temporary teams. They have to do with how the team is shaped physically, how they shape their early social structure, or a combination of the two.

First, whenever possible, the workplaces of a temporary team's members should be changed so that they are close together and really *look* like a team, both to the rest of the organization and to themselves. This will make the likelihood of informal contacts (and therefore getting to know one another) much greater than if they spend most of their time ensconced in their old offices.

Second, if the team members still retain significant parallel duties with their old groups, then they should, if possible, have two workplaces, their old one and one that's located with the other members of the temporary team.

Third, barring new workplaces for individuals (because of space or cost restrictions), there should at least be a *team* workplace designated. It needs to be an area that can accommodate formal and informal contacts and be a central repository for files, other information sources, and symbols of the team's existence and purpose (e.g., plans, drawings, statement of purpose, pictures of the members, diagrams of the team's relationships with other organizational units, announcements, progress charts or diagrams, or whatever). A team that has no spot of its own has a very hard time establishing a strong sense of identity in its members. It is worth setting up such a place no matter how tight the organization is for space. Not doing this is tantamount to saying it doesn't matter whether this team performs well or not, and if that is the case, it is probably not worth bothering to set the team up at all.

Fourth, the team's workplace should have a variety of spots within it, including a common meeting area and some places for individuals to get off by themselves, undisturbed by members or outsiders. It should also have materials and supplies so that members do not need to hunt for such simple items as paper, pens, easels, typewriters, and the like. These materials and the layout of the team's workplace should be chosen for the specific tasks and modes of working of that team, rather than be simply a duplication of what is given to the average group in the organization. The team should not just take what is assigned to it and make do.

Fifth, in terms of building a sense of identity and teamwork early in a temporary team's life, one good group activity task is to work together on shaping the team's physical setting. The members get a lot more mileage from this than if the task is done for them. This task helps to identify differences in perceived mission, expectations about each other and how they will work together, and so on. It requires a definition of goals, tasks, and modes of working and gives the members a chance to have a successful experience together at problem solving and implementing solutions. It is an excellent team development activity because it is centered around a concrete task with visible results, and because it tends to promote a norm of shaping the team's own fate, rather than just accepting and reacting to what others give to it.

Sixth, another related early task would be to do some climate-building: to openly discuss the norms the members bring to the team, to identify differences due to different backgrounds, and to identify a set of norms that will be most useful for what they are going to do as a temporary team. This will usually entail individuals' letting go of some of their inappropriate expectations, plus the creation of some new, necessary norms that are missing.[1]

Lastly, it is important for a temporary team to set up clear communication links with those other parts of the organization or the surrounding environment with whom it most needs to have contacts. This may be done through installing electronic hookups, scheduling regular crossgroup meetings, choosing a team location adjacent to relevant groups, or arranging to have access to joint facilities (eating, copying, physical fitness, and so on), which will naturally promote interaction. I have seen temporary teams develop a strong sense of internal identity but forget to establish these links, thereby cutting themselves off from many of the realities of their tasks.

These are some ways in which a newly formed temporary team can work on both its own process and its relationship with its surroundings. The point is not that these are meant to be a substitute for clear thinking and good knowledge of the content of what the team is doing. It is rather that the physical setting and social norms of the team can often be an invisible key to group development, so that early attention to ecological details is valuable if the team is to have its best chance of success and the experience is to be satisfying for its members.

IMPROVED APPROACHES TO TRAINING AND DEVELOPMENT

All work organizations need to have their members engage in developmental, learning activities as well as productive tasks. The settings for such learning experiences vary, from makeshift events in the one conference room in the building to programs conducted in campus-type educational centers. Most organizations of any size eventually create

---

[1]For a full discussion of how to describe, analyze, and change a group's norms, see F. Steele and S. Jenks, *The Feel of the Workplace* (Reading, Mass.: Addison-Wesley, 1977), ch. 4–5.

development settings dedicated to training and educational activities for part or all of the organization. Some of these settings work well, many are mediocre, and quite a few are poor for the purposes they are supposed to serve. However, because the basic tasks can be well specified for such a facility, it should be possible to do a good job of designing it and setting up helpful processes for using and managing it. Having worked in the areas of executive and management development for almost twenty years, I think about this design problem from the standpoints of both designers and users. This discussion will cover some of the generalizations that have emerged from my experiences and the observation of many organizational educational centers in action.

Location

Many training facilities are located in spaces that have not been needed or claimed by any other unit of the organization. The facilities are jerry-rigged to suit the new function. There is little conscious attention to locational issues: Should the facility be central, visible, and accessible so as to communicate the importance of continuing personal development to the long-term health of the organization? Or should it be removed, separate, and nonvisible in order to provide a "cultural island" where people are freer to think in new ways by being removed from the usual day-to-day inputs and scrutiny of other members of the organization? Each of these types of location has its advantages and disadvantages. The point is to choose a location that relates to criteria specific to what will be done there. By contrast, many training units create a setting by (a) taking over leftover space (because they have low power in the system) or (b) creating a very flashy training center that is elegant but far removed (physically and symbolically) from the rest of the organization and therefore not a good setting for stimulating people to think about how to deal with the issues they live with day-to-day.

Features of the Setting

The nature of the educational facilities obviously should depend on the kinds of training and educational activities that will take place there. Technical training facilities will usually require a setting with visual aids, equipment, tools, materials to practice with, and sufficient space for students to practice their new skills. My experience suggests that it is better in the long run to have too much space, equipment, and/or material rather than too little, since the major cumulative cost in training is the time of the people involved, not the materials. The people who experience dead periods while waiting for a chance to practice cost an organization money, as opposed to the marketplace situation where the customer may bear the cost of waiting if the production facility is running at capacity. Always "running at capacity" in skill training sessions may seem like an efficient use of resources, but probably it means the facility is not large enough for the tasks being done.

For supervisory and management training, the setting tends to be less technical but no less important. There should usually be a variety of sizes of spaces accommodating small to large (forty or more people) groups. Furniture such as tables and chairs should not be fixed in place but should allow flexible arrangements. This allows layouts to be quickly changed as different programs use the spaces, as well as allowing modifications when basic methods of instruction are changing over time. To me the most depressing educational setting is one where teaching and learning modes are dictated by an unchangeable physical layout, such as an auditorium-type room with rows of bolted-down, tiered seats that require lecture-type presentations.

I should also mention here the importance of the most mundane feature of all — the washrooms for men and women. I can testify from sad and frustrating experiences that the rhythm or flow of many programs can be ruined by too few bathrooms or ones located too far from where you are meeting. Every break becomes a too-long experience of frustration that affects the session following it and dilutes concentration on the issues at hand. As an example, consider this description of a key officer education center of the U.S. Air Force:

> The auditorium will seat at least 800, but the building does not have rest room facilities for classes of that size. The result is that you have to take long breaks between sessions, to fit facilities to class size. When the building was built the engineers, or whoever controlled design, defined it as a *public building* and said you could only have a certain number of stalls, urinals, etc. based on approved limits for public buildings in general. The university people said that the design should reflect the educational mission, but lost out.

Visual Aids

This is an interesting specific feature of educational centers, and the possibilities run from the simplicity of a chalkboard or easel with paper through overhead and film projectors to sophisticated equipment for multimedia presentations, simultaneous live and tape shows, and the like. Again, my experience has been that the most usable features tend to be portable items such as easels, pads, projectors, and TV monitors that can be set up easily in varying locations depending on a group's size and the desired configuration. There are many ways to use visual aids besides presentations to a passive audience, but fixed equipment tends to shape events into such presentations and make the experience fit the equipment rather than vice versa.

The walls of a meeting and training room also qualify in my mind as a visual aid, *if* it is possible to use them for displays, keeping track of what ideas have been produced (by sticking up newsprint sheets), and the like. To this end, some of the best training spaces from my point of view as an educator have been those with clear wall spaces covered in burlap or corkboard so that materials can be easily pinned up or taken down without concern about damaging the walls. Conversely, plaster or sheetrock walls tend to inhibit such easy display, as do walls with lots of "nice" panelling and other decorations. The general training assumption behind clear, usable wall space is the value of keeping ideas, products, and issues visible in the room so that people's minds continue to be stimulated by them even when they are daydreaming and letting their eyes just wander around the room.

Creating Feedback Loops

My final point is not related to how you physically set up the training setting, but how you set up the social conditions that allow you to assess the setting's appropriateness and improve it when the need arises. My recommendation is to build in regular data collections from both participants and staff, relating to both the content of the events held there and their perceptions of the effects of the physical setting on these events. A simple evaluation form at the close of a session is one way to do it, especially if supplemented periodically with an informal group interview with participants and staff of a program or course.

There are two benefits from taking the trouble to do regular evaluations. One is that in most work organizations training and development activities must be experienced by users as being satisfactory or managers will not send or allow people to attend programs, or they will look to outside sources for developmental activities. The second benefit is simply that it makes sense for an entity devoted to learning and development to represent those goals in its own process. There is often an odd sort of mixed message transmitted by a corporate training facility trying to help people to learn and at the same time creating no mechanism whereby the management and staff of the facility can learn and make changes based on their experiences. Conversely, training events conducted with a spirit of inquiry into their aptness and impact will tend to support a spirit of inquiry and curiosity in the participants. I believe that such a spirit is vital if people are to continue to learn through their careers.

Key Areas of Choice

One way of summarizing my notions about the design of training centers is to close this section with a list of the "watershed issues" that I use to help clients determine the shape and feel of the institution they want to create. I have found that a training group that openly answers these questions and deals with the disagreements they tend to uncover will generally end up with a better, more consciously designed facility than a group that simply bases a design on an aggregate of their past experiences with training facilities.

1. *Central identity.* What will this unit *be*, and how can this be expressed in the design of the setting? What features should particularly be avoided because they would conflict with this identity?
2. *Basic activities.* What are the various events that will happen here, and what features are needed in order to make them go well?
3. *Underlying assumptions.* What are the basic assumptions and theories about how people learn that will underlie what we will do in the new setting (e.g., how much will we emphasize lectures and presentations, group discussions, participative experiences, and so on)? What settings, resources, and mixes of people will best mirror these assumptions?
4. *Structured and unstructured use.* Are we designing this facility to present only organized programs, or do we also want to provide a resource center where people could come and experiment, engaging in self-directed learning activities using the setting's resources?
5. *Efficiency.* Assuming we have limited resources, how can we use them to the greatest effect (e.g., if there are permanent staff, do we have to provide offices for everyone or could we experiment with a tighter, more flexible arrangement)?
6. *Social relations.* How do we want the various kinds of people who will use this center to interact or relate to each other (permanent staff, visiting faculty, students, visitors)? What does this suggest about design and location of such magnet facilities as lounges, coffee areas, and bathrooms?
7. *Community.* To what extent do we want to create physical boundaries in the layout of spaces so that programs are felt to be separate entities, versus designing overlapping spaces that tend to draw peo-

ple into feeling that they are part of the training center community as a whole?

8. *Symbolic cues.*   To what extent must we conform to the organization's policies and norms concerning status symbols in office design, versus being able to create settings based mainly on other functional dimensions? More broadly, how much are we trying to mirror the norms and values of the organization's culture versus creating an alternative culture that stimulates people to think in new ways about issues in work and management?

I am not saying that answering these questions automatically provides a concrete design for a corporate training/educational facility. But I do believe that if such questions are *not* asked and answered when such a facility is created, it will tend to serve its purposes moderately but not exceptionally well, and will not be much of a force for long-term development and growth for the organization and its members.

OFFICES AND NEW TECHNOLOGY

Another opportunity (or actually, essential area) for the application of an organizational ecology viewpoint is in the design and use of white-collar office workplaces incorporating the rapidly expanding array of new equipment. Sometimes called "the office of the future" or "the integrated office," such installations have a wide range of new technology to choose from: word-processing systems, new reproduction systems, computer graphics, information storage systems such as high-capacity, small-sized computer memories, sophisticated telephone and video systems, closed-circuit television links for teleconferencing (and reducing travel), computer teleconferencing capabilities, and electronic mail systems. The key issue I want to address here is not equipment per se, but rather the necessity to coordinate innovations in office technology with social and physical system changes. It is important to introduce new technology because it supports the users, not just because it exists and allows managers to feel that they will automatically be effective if their offices are up-to-date.

It stands to reason that if all these new office work systems are grafted onto old office area layouts their impact will tend to be diminished in many instances. Without asking the necessary questions about redesign, the outcomes will essentially be left to chance. A more logical strategy is to determine what kind of work is done in the office, how it is done, and what technological developments can change the basic methods or improve the productivity of the methods that are used. Having made some preliminary determination of promising new directions in equipment or work processes, analyses should be made of the work setting in terms of (a) what layouts will maximize the payoff of the changes and allow people to take best advantage of them, and (b) what effects these technologies will have on the users and on the social system as a whole. The workplace should be designed to emphasize the positive effects and minimize the negative ones as best it can. The goal is to create *integrated systems* of people, policies, technologies, and physical settings that can be combined effectively in the processes at the heart of most office-type operations: information acquisition, information processing, information storage, decision making, and transmittal.

There are a number of useful approaches to achieving this type of integrated office ecology. One example is the "Work Design in Offices" study developed in a large international corporation by Bill Bevans and his associates in the Corporate Human Resources group.[2] They have been involved in improving the utilization and impact of word-processing equipment and new communication technologies in the secretarial/clerical areas and in enhancing managers' abilities to use and manage the outputs of these functions. They start with the assumption that not all departments in the organization are alike; they have different types of work, different stresses on them, and different needs for office technology and new methods. Bevans emphasizes a focus on four areas of potential leverage within each department:

1. *Work design* — how tasks and processes are organized.
2. *Equipment and layout* — the fit between technical systems and the physical setting.
3. *Procedures* — the extent to which defined responsibilities, role expectations, and work procedures are congruent with the work design.
4. *Behavior patterns* — the nature of regular actions and interactions among workers, managers, visitors, and other groups.

The actual process involves working out an individual study plan for each department, with the lead and facilitative role taken by human resource specialists. Although details vary, the key feature of the plan is the involvement of the department's workers themselves in developing and carrying out the study and utilizing its results in a process of planned change. The steps that are typically involved include establishing im-

---

[2]The description here is based in part on a memorandum by Bevans called "Work Design in Offices," written in September 1980.

provement objectives, describing the work done in the department, analyzing requirements, specifying technological opportunities, identifying
barriers to getting the work done (from their own points of view), developing recommendations for specific issues or areas, implementing
changes (improved technology, changed layouts, training, new procedures), and setting up and using a self-monitoring system to check progress on productivity and satisfaction with changes.

The specific changes that have been implemented to date with the
support of human resources and services staff people range from very simple to relatively complex: changing chairs and lighting placement, designing new work stations for specific tasks, changing the placement and
capacity of storage units, introducing advanced word-processing units,
grouping word-processing functions in one area, creating a central community space with information storage as a magnet to draw users, installing sound absorbers for "hot spots" of high noise reflectivity, changing
the procedures for handling incoming messages so that they collect at a
central spot rather than at individual work stations, and using this center
as a clearinghouse for information about members' whereabouts.

These efforts have typically produced results such as better balanced
secretarial/clerical services to departmental users, better product quality (accuracy, appearance, layout), shorter turnaround time, increased
productivity at some staff levels, plus reduced use of temporary help and
overtime work. In addition, the process has tended to generate a high
degree of pride and sense of ownership on the part of operators using new
technology.

Bevans and his human resource specialists believe that these results
more than justify their view that the office environment of the 1980s must
be planned and managed with the same degree of logic (although not necessarily the same assumptions) as a well-designed manufacturing facility. Opportunities generally exist in any office work setting to innovate
in technology, workplace design, and procedures for doing the work itself.
The process described here of work analysis and redesign by the working group itself seems to have a lot to recommend it, both in terms of
generating commitment to the changes and in terms of using live data
from real users of the setting, not just someone else's projections of what
users ought to be experiencing. However, this process may or may not
fit well with the style of a given organization. If it does not, then some
other process can be used, as long as it is kept in mind that the process
should be an integrated one that

1. Describes tasks as they are now
2. Describes how they should or could be organized differently

3. Designs new mixes of technology to support the tasks
4. Designs new workplaces to fit the tasks, technology, and needs of the users
5. Suggests and implements new policies, norms, and procedures (behavioral systems) that make the best use of new technology and layouts
6. Provides appropriate training experiences to help workers make changes effectively and with little slippage

The theme to remember during this process is that the new technology is a *tool*, not the purpose of the office installation. If this is not clear, employees will resist even simple changes due to feeling driven out of their jobs or being treated as second-class to the machinery.[3]

Frank Duffy and his associates in the London design firm DEGW have recently evaluated another key part of office redesign: the problems associated with incorporating new technology into existing buildings. In a European multicompany study called ORBIT,[4] which is soon to be followed up in the United States, they considered a number of design dimensions that need to be addressed when redoing existing office settings: light level and sources, temperature control, noise control, power supply (physical distribution around the building), power stability, furniture dimensions, flexibility for changing workplace layouts, and ease of day-to-day management and maintenance.

Some of the consistent qualities they found in buildings best able to cope with new information technology were good local control of air conditioning with many zones; the ability to upgrade the capacity of the structure through both space and accessibility; medium depth allowing natural light to 60 percent or more of the offices; perimeter design allowing for increased office separation when appropriate; and the ability to accommodate large quantities of cabling, with frequent outlets.[5]

The results of the U.S. study should be of great interest to anyone concerned about the office of the future. Elaborate systems are not worth much if they cannot be incorporated into the physical setting without great costs or inefficiencies.

---

[3]For an extensive discussion of such change strategies, see Calvin Pava, *Managing New Office Technology* (New York: Free Press, 1983).

[4]Francis Duffy, principal author, "The ORBIT Project: Findings, Conclusions, and Recommendations," published by Duffy, Ely, Giffone, and Worthington (DEGW), 8–9 Bulstrode Place, London W1M 5FW, UK, January 1983.

[5]See Duffy, "The ORBIT Project," pp. 93–94.

SOCIAL ENGINEERING IN CHANGING LAYOUTS

One of the ORBIT study themes is the possible shift from the open-plan layout back toward more separate offices. This is opposite to a consistent trend over the last twenty years toward fewer closed, fixed office spaces. With this trend in mind, my final application example is not a physical design but a social system redesign to complement a physical change. The example is the shift from a closed, "cellular" layout of private offices with walls and doors to a more open, flowing plan where people have workplaces or workstations but these are designated not by walls but by screens, furniture arrangements, plants, and the like. Many white-collar, office-type facilities have shifted in this direction over the past twenty years in response to a number of forces: the increasing rate of change in the organizations' environments, which requires a more flexible, adaptable approach to layouts than the cellular office complex provides; the increasing cost of building materials, which emphasizes the advantages of reusable, less permanent installations; and a shift in management philosophy in many organizations away from well-defined, prescribed interactions between positions or levels, toward a more fluid, open communication pattern based on current information needs and sources rather than predetermined "proper channels."

All these forces push office design toward less fixed, more changeable open plans that facilitate both increased interaction levels and easier tinkering with layouts. It does not make much sense to build a highly structured office complex and either adapt the organization's work patterns to fit that structure or to spend large amounts of money to tear it out and rebuild as system needs change. Along with this trend has come a new set of problems associated with the new layout patterns. The open layout is often not a satisfactory place to spend one's work time. The noise level is high, distracting, or both. People may communicate more frequently but about less consequential topics out of fear of being overheard. Design decisions about adjacent areas are often taken with no coordination of their effects on each other. People sometimes feel exposed and vulnerable, as well as powerless to do anything about it. As companies move toward more open layouts, their members often experience (and express) a rising sense of dissatisfaction and discomfort.

It is my belief that these problems are the result of a lack of follow-up support for the design changes: no training, no attempts to consciously develop new norms about social behavior in the new spaces, and few or no changes in management and supervisory style. What has been lacking is the use of social-change technologies to accompany the physical-change effort so that the ecological system can be rebalanced. While this need has been little recognized in office planning, it has been more obvious in creating factories and other physically oriented task settings where training in coordination, decision making, and use of new tools and control mechanisms has been considered a natural part of engineering the change process. For office installations there seems to have been an implicit assumption that workers already knew what they needed to know, so that there was no necessity for training and social change efforts.

In short, I believe that many of the negative experiences associated with open-plan offices are the result of what we might call the "half-trial syndrome": doing a physical change without trying to effect the complementary support, training, and new social designs that would be useful in making the new layout succeed; the new layout is then evaluated as having "failed." Managers would not do just half the things they needed to do when introducing a new product or engineering a new production system; yet they will repeatedly do this in the realm of office facilities.

So, when someone says that their new open layout does not "work," what might the contributing causes be? One could be that the layout is not, in fact, very functional for the tasks and the people involved. A second might be that the social norms of the users' groups are rooted in the demands of more closed offices and lead to problems in areas such as control of intrusions and noise. A third cause could be that the system's control policies tend to block real adaptation by the users, so that they cannot realize the potential satisfactions from the new spaces (e.g., they are forbidden to personalize their own work spots). A fourth cause might be that managerial and supervisory processes also have not been altered to fit the new layouts. Subordinates may feel embarrassed or exploited by the ways their bosses treat them in full view of peers, and the bosses feel constrained by their own visibility.

The last three factors are all potentially influenceable by social change technologies in the applied behavioral sciences aimed at such targets as group norms, management skills in decision making and problem solving, and structuring effective feedback loops.

For example, a group moving into an open or modified open layout could do an analysis of their present norms about social interactions, identifying three categories of norms: old norms to be kept as useful in the new layout as well, old norms that should be dropped because they do not fit the new layout, and new norms that are missing now but would be useful in the new layout. Table 16.1 shows a few simple examples from such an analysis.

A similar analysis can be done for the more formal, written policies about spatial behavior, use of common facilities, personalization of one's own work area, and so on. (For instance, it becomes *more* important,

Table 16.1:

Changing Norms with a Changed Layout

Behavior Areas	Effective Norm in Closed Layout	Effective Norm in Open Layout
Voice level	Lower in common areas; whatever you like in your own office	Lower in common areas and in own workplace or will be intrusive to others
Greeting people when you see them	Say hello when see them- it's impolite not to do so	Possibly say hello first time seen that day, but no more or you'll always be greeting each other
Entering someone's space	OK to do it unless door is closed; respect closed door as signal to stay out	OK to do it unless some signal is up saying "I'm in my private mode" (and norm should be to respect these signals)
Where to chat with people	Any hallway or common area is OK	Shouldn't chat right on top of someone else's workspace - forces them to be a part of the conversation even if they don't want to be
Talking on telephone	Talk as loudly as you like if your door is shut	Modulate your voice level so as not to blast out others around you
Use of radios	Personal option in own office	Group issue if others can hear it in your area

not less, that policies in an open-plan layout support personalization of one's immediate work environment.) Both the formal and informal rules and patterns can support users' needs in several ways: providing needed privacy and a sense of territoriality in the absence of traditional control mechanisms such as walls and doors, and doing this without negating the positive features of the open layout (e.g., without cramming in a mass of filing cabinets as substitutes for walls); supporting innovative methods of creating personal places in a nontraditional layout; encouraging employees to use the opportunities and flexibility of the new layouts; and helping them transform bland, no-person's lands into interesting, vital common spaces used by all occupants of the facility.

This example is meant to encourage an awareness of the half-trial problem and to point out the need for a follow-through on the total design effort, taking into account the organization's total ecological pattern. It is not intended to be a pitch for open-plan layouts per se, since a similar process should occur when changing from open to a more closed plan. Although I mentioned factors that tend to push toward the open plan, there are many groups that can function just as well or better in a more traditional closed-office layout, especially where relatively little spontaneous interaction is required and the layouts change infrequently. But the point about the need for an integrated sociophysical design still holds, since most groups working in closed layouts also suffer from inappropriate or outmoded rules and norms. The thrust just happens to be different: the need to provide new controls on stimulation in open layouts, and the need to stimulate contacts and integration in closed layouts. Each social system need tends to be the complement to the dominant pattern encouraged by the physical system design.

CHAPTER 17

Workplace Design and Management in the Future

This final chapter has two purposes: to speculate about some of the most interesting (and in some cases most likely) future directions in the design and management of work settings, especially those factors that are likely to shape such settings; and to review the most important assumptions and principles of the organizational ecology viewpoint that I have been working with throughout the book.

FUTURE TRENDS

There are so many work settings in the United States that it is very hard for someone to ever see more than a tiny fraction of them. We also tend to hear about only the most striking or visible ones, which leaves 99.5 percent of the others to be experienced only by their users. In addition, it is hard at a given point in time to see exactly what the *patterns* are in the changes that are going on in a field such as workplace design. Working within these limitations, I will discuss some of the indicators of future directions that seem relatively clear from my own perspective.

Changing User Expectations

On the average, I think organizational members in this country are becoming more aware of their surroundings, of their own needs and values, and of the impact of settings on the satisfaction of such needs. They are less willing to leave the shaping of their immediate environment to others. This in turn leads to more challenge to organizational leaders to create or support work settings that do better at serving both organizational and individual needs, and to establish policies and rules that support individuality and expressiveness in people's own work areas. There will also be increasing pressure from lower level employees for more op-

186

portunities to participate in environmental decisions. This is partly fallout from other participative management trends and partly the result of increased awareness of process and desire for a more alive work experience. There is also a discernible change in the kinds of place needs that workers express, away from stereotyped concern for the symbolic status elements toward more varied desires for environmental features to satisfy task, pleasure, change, social, and growth needs.

New Diagnosis and Assessment Methods

In order for employees' increased environmental awareness to result in systemic improvements in workplace design, organizational leaders will have to set up better sensing processes for gauging the quality of the matches between users and work settings. There is a fair amount of experimentation in this area today, and I would expect it to increase over the next few years. Some of the methods that are likely to be used more frequently are regular employee surveys, "hot lines" to report workplace problems, a suggestion box for members' ideas about problems or solutions related to the workplace, rotating committees that periodically collect data on the appropriateness and usefulness of the work environment, videotape or film assessments done in the workplace and then studied by both members and professionals to identify areas for fruitful change or upgrading, regular visits by consultants to interview and observe users in their workplaces, and periodic reviews by management of the patterns and needs of the system in relation to the physical setting. All these, and other methods as well, will tend to become "business as usual" mechanisms in the future, rather than just being done when someone gets totally fed up with the design of the workplace, as is often the case today.

Creative Retrofitting

This is a natural step that moves from regular diagnosis of setting quality to regular rehabilitation and updating of that setting. We are in the middle of a major societal change from a culture of abundance and waste to one of scarce resources with a necessity for better utilization of those we have. There will be more organizations that will develop policies of periodic review and upgrading of their places rather than just building or renting new space when spatial problems can no longer be ignored by the leadership. Doing more with what we have is an ethic that is on the rise in the United States, although many cultures, such as the Europeans, Japanese, and Chinese, are far ahead of us.

As a result, U.S. organizations will be forced to do more regular

audits of their work settings. This, in turn, will lead to a process of regular
maintenance and renewal, but the process will be defined much more
broadly than the traditional attention to maintenance of the most obvious
physical features such as floors, walls, carpets, drapes, heating systems,
and so on. Maintenance will be an issue concerning interaction patterns,
usefulness of conference rooms and other community spaces, entrances
and exits, traffic patterns, sign usage, symbolic identification of group
areas, proximities of individuals and groups to each other, and so on.
These will all be considered part of management's general responsibility
to cycle through the assessment and renewal process as a part of maintaining a healthy organization.

Integration of Workplace Management and Organization Development

Over the last fifteen years, many American work organizations have
developed an internal resource group loosely called organization development (OD). It usually includes behavioral-science-trained staff people
who are tasked with assessing, maintaining, or developing the organization as a healthy human system that is able to fulfill its mission, adapt
to a changing environment, and maintain a healthy climate for its members. From an ecological perspective, one of the elements to which internal OD groups should pay attention is the quality of the physical environment, both for members' satisfaction and for task accomplishment.
In practice there has tended to be relatively little connection between
social system OD activities and the processes that organizational leaders
use to control and change the physical environment. I expect that this
connection will (and should) become much stronger. OD practitioners
will concern themselves with organizational ecology as one aspect of
healthy organizations; facilities and maintenance groups will become
more aware of both the organizational and human implications of what
they are doing and the potential contributions that the OD professionals
can make to such work. The result will be a more natural integration,
with a broader viewpoint for both groups, as well as some interesting implications for organization development activities.

Management of Organizational Ecology at the Corporate Level

Some very interesting trends are developing in the place-manage-
ment process of large, multisite corporations that must be regularly creating or altering work settings because of their growth or increasing com-

plexity. My work in a number of such organizations suggests that most have tended to deal with their ecological pattern on a piecemeal, one-place-at-a-time basis. I think there will be a shift toward top executive involvement in developing a *corporate organizational ecology strategy* that looks at the pattern of the *whole* as well as the characteristics and shape of the individual parts or sites. This is a particularly crucial development for rapid-growth organizations that are continually expanding their number of sites, since workplace development becomes one of the most regular tasks. They need to look at this development in a coordinated manner so that good patterns of sociophysical relationships become reinforced and negative ones are eliminated.

If this focus becomes natural for the leaders of a corporation, they will begin to develop a corporate organizational ecology philosophy that would cover issues as varied as when to own and when to rent, where to locate and when to move, how to develop effective management talents for facilities planning and alterations, and how to create space policies that stimulate rather than strangle creativity and adaptation.

The awareness of organizational ecology at the top of an organization is also a big step toward a similar viewpoint being taken at other levels of the organization. If the corporate executive group also applies the notions of executive team ecology to itself, this does even more to reinforce the value of thinking of the people and places of the organization as an integrated system (see Chapter 15).

Reconnecting Home and Workplace

In many sections of the United States, the trend in the twentieth century has been toward greater physical separation of home and workplace, so that people's family lives tend to be disintegrated. When materials, land, and transportation are all relatively cheap, this may make some economic sense (if not psychological). But as scarcity becomes a bigger factor for all three of these, we will see a trend toward concentration rather than physical dispersion in community design, toward closeness of work and home settings such as in nineteenth-century New England mill towns. We probably have already passed the maximum dispersion point by five to ten years (at least in the eastern half of the United States) and are headed back toward greater concentration.

This trend also implies that there is a need for more attention to workplace design and use policies that allow overlap between home and work settings — recreational facilities, regular visits, places for families to come and see the work setting, and a community-center-type feeling to major employers in a town. Along with this will go company policies that encourage visits and use of company settings by the families of employees or other members of the community. Methods to encourage these changes include designing layouts to make it easy for visitors to be around without interfering with work processes, holding events for families in the workplace itself (not in some irrelevant public park), and changing work hours (such as flex-time) to allow people to control the pattern of their presence at home and work settings. Another design feature that might encourage a home-work connection would be using people's families as a theme in decorations and graphics.

WHAT IS IMPORTANT?

In a sense, my purpose in writing this book and in doing my consulting on organizational ecology is to shape the future of American work life in directions that make sense to me and fit my values. My own conclusions, generalizations, and biases therefore represent one way of describing the future of organizational ecology as I think it should be and as I am trying to make it. These generalizations have been scattered throughout this book and in some cases have been implied in the discussion rather than stated directly. It therefore seems that a useful way to provide some closure to my views on organizational ecology and its potential for improving workplace design and management would be to summarize the key guiding principles that make the most sense to me. I have grouped these principles into two main groups: those dealing with design and layout choices, and those concerned with social system processes that result in both design choices and patterns of use of workplaces.

Design and Layout Generalizations

There is no single "best" design for factory or office layouts—what is appropriate depends on the mix of people, the tasks being done, the resources available, and the stage of development of the system.

Visibility is a very important feature of layout and design; it tends to build a sense of identity and vitality in a workplace and is usually (but not always) a desirable feature of layouts.

Having an *integrated decor* that expresses an identity for the overall system is an important part of generating a sense of place in both members and visitors. On the other hand, *personalization of workplaces* is also important and helps people to establish and maintain their own sense of identity within the larger whole. The decor should allow both overall themes and individual variations to be expressed.

Privacy and sense of community are both fundamental human needs, and good designs allow people to achieve both in their day-to-day lives. The "cave and court" design discussed in Chapter 15, with a small withdrawal space and a larger communal area, seems to meet these needs fairly well.

Office areas need central community spaces that serve as gathering points, as *centers* for the system so that people can find out what is happening and feel that there is a place where action happens in the system.

Traffic patterns, entrances, and exits should be carefully thought out and designed, since they shape people's *sequences of experience* in the system. They sometimes make more difference than do individual workplaces, especially if they are done with little thought.

Orientational elements are a key feature of work settings. Signs and other graphics help people tell where they are in relation to where they want to go (such as the visual information available to people when they step into lobbies on different floors of high-rise office buildings). Pictures, signs, diagrams, and the like can all help, and their absence implies that organizational leaders do not care whether or not members and visitors have a good experience in this setting.

Whenever possible, it is good to avoid the creation of *no-person's lands*—those bland, undecorated zones that lie between various groups' territories and have no character to them whatsoever. People tend to turn themselves off when passing through such zones.

The notion of *scarce resources* should be taken seriously in terms of amenities in the workplace. For example, the walls with external windows should be thought of as a scarce resource to be owned by the community, not as private vistas. The value question here is whether this scarce resource (light and views) is "owned" by only high-ranking members or by the members of the system as a whole.

The emphasis on *status symbols* as a determinant of workplace features and location should be minimized or controlled, so that greater layout flexibility can be achieved.

There should be institutional support for *quick personalization* of workplaces by those people who are temporarily assigned to a workplace. Lacking this support, many members of an organization always feel like visitors or temporary guests rather than residents of their systems, and they never feel they have a right to make themselves at home.

Flexibility is a buzz-word that gets used in many different ways but is in fact a crucial dimension to consider when shaping workplaces in a fast-changing organization. Sizes of spaces, arrangements of furniture, relative locations of people and facilities, sizes of group areas, users of areas—all these, if kept open for variations, allow the organization to do more with a given amount of physical resources.

Providing *forums* is also very important. This is a key feature that is missing in many organizations. Forums are settings where people can gather, and see and hear one another discuss issues that are shared but have no place to be discussed as part of day-to-day work activities.

Graphics should be thought of as a medium that can tie settings together and create patterns of experiences for their users. They can be alive and catch the theme of a setting, and especially be useful in the focal points (e.g., end walls of corridors) that tend to get forgotten as no-person's lands yet get looked at a lot.

When locations for people and groups are determined, *functional distances* should be the key. The accessibility of getting from one point to another should be considered, regardless of the physical distance.

Boundaries should be thought about and designed consciously: how permeable or fixed should the boundaries between groups be, how can this be expressed physically, and when should the thickness of boundaries be changed?

Sizes of areas and spaces need to be carefully chosen. More is not necessarily better, although it is usually treated as just an economic issue: create as much space as the budget will allow. Work settings should not be so small and dense that they feel overcrowded for the types of tasks and users, nor so large and sparsely populated that people do not feel a sense of vitality.

Materials chosen for walls, floors, furniture, and so on often end up influencing a wide range of user behaviors in the setting. In general, materials should be chosen so as not to inhibit the potential uses of the setting. They should get better with use and wear, not degenerate and become shabby (the fear of which leads to the institution of very constraining rules about use). The criterion should be that they can be maintained given hard use. There should also be sound-absorbing materials in high-noise areas, as well as plants and other fabrics to soften hard surfaces.

Social Processes for Design and Use Control

A number of other principles that have been mentioned or alluded to throughout this book are less related to specific design solutions than they are to the ways in which such solutions are achieved and the ways such solutions' uses are controlled by the social system of the organization.

Top leadership members should clarify for themselves the different *classes of decisions* that go into creating new or improved workplaces. They should decide how comfortable they are with unilateral versus shared decision making in each class — when should users make inputs, when should they actually make the decisions. This is generally better than undifferentiated, unilateral decision processes where the top level holds nominal power over all classes of decisions (which results in many low-quality, low-acceptance decisions), as long as a good structure is developed so the process does not become too slow and cumbersome.

The same principle holds for lower-level groups within the organization. I believe in creating an overall guiding framework, then having groups take responsibility for their destiny within this framework. This tends to produce decisions that are more reality centered, to build teamwork within the groups, and to reinforce the concept of workplace management as an ongoing responsibility of managers at various levels in the hierarchy.

As I described in the first part of this chapter, I believe in *regular data collections and diagnoses* of the match between human system needs and physical settings. This provides an ongoing health-maintenance approach versus curing or solving problems only when things become obviously diseased.

I also believe in capitalizing on the *potential* of settings. Policies and management evaluations and responsibilities should encourage people to use a setting with gusto rather than with timidity. Controls should support doing primary tasks well, rather than aim at least-cost maintenance, unless the business of the system is actually to demonstrate least-cost maintenance of settings.

For a new workplace, *full use* means avoiding the "plastic on the furniture" syndrome, whereby all sorts of rules are developed to maintain the setting in its move-in state. Trying to maintain the place as it was when brand new tends to block free use of it to do the real business of the system, not to mention the fact that it is not even a good experience for the members. They do not feel the sense of ownership until it has some traces of human beings in it.

Organizational leaders should encourage the *open resolution of conflicts* in spatial decision areas. The immediacy of such conflict can build conflict resolution skills, if there is high-level support and pressure to work these issues through. It also leads to interesting joint uses of common facilities, which tend to be underutilized if conflicts are avoided or covered up.

Periodic assessments of social norms will determine how well they match the physical setting — do they allow people to really use the potential of the workplace? These assessments can lead to the development of strategies to bring about physical change, social change, or a combination of the two. A regular issue to be addressed is what social norm changes are necessary when technological and physical changes are made in a work group.

There should also be a conscious effort on the part of top management to design social structures that support and encourage *individual problem solving* of and *adaptations* to work environments, especially right after moving into a new setting. (Many organizations set up facilities management groups that are rewarded for discouraging such adaptations and keeping users from having any impact on their workplaces.)

When *designing organizational events*, the choice of a setting and how it can be used should always be kept consciously in mind as making a difference. This leads to experimentation with where events are held, the sequences of experiences in how people get there, symbolic messages that are transmitted by the location, memories people bring with them from past events in that spot, and so on. The point is to make more conscious use of the potency of settings' images and not to get stuck in holding events in the same old locations just because they are handy or traditional.

CONCLUSIONS

I hope that at a bare minimum one message has come through loud and clear throughout this book: my excitement about the organizational ecology viewpoint and its ability to provide a useful perspective on many mundane choices and decisions that tend to be made independently and with little thought to the impact on one another and on the organization as an organic system. Much of the interaction effect of physical and social systems today tends to take place at a partly conscious and partly unconscious level. It can only be influenced in those management groups where it is "fashionable" to be concerned about such things, even though it has just as big an impact (and often more, in the negative direction) in those where it is not an accepted area of concern and attention.

The potential I see here, and which I have been trying to encourage in this book, is for managers and group members to take a bigger role in shaping their relations with their settings, through both physical design of the settings and social design of policies and informal norms about behavior in those settings. I feel very strongly that the top-level executives and middle-level managers should both take an ecological perspective when thinking about what they are influencing and what influences them as they do their work. This is part of what affects their results and satisfaction, as well as that of those who are members of the organizations they control. As such, it should be an arena for much more conscious discussion and experimentation than has typically been the case in American work organizations.

The same need holds true from a total system or corporate perspective. Since creating, changing, and getting rid of settings is one of the most frequent actions of most large corporations, the executive group should develop a philosophy of their own about what shape they want the system to assume, how they want to manage their settings, how they will handle growth and decline in size or complexity, symbolic style guidelines that will project messages about the system's identity, classes of decisions they want to hold onto versus decisions to be delegated to lower levels, and how they want to shape their own executive work space so as to affect their ecology as an executive team. All these strands should be woven into a fabric of workplace management processes that ensure a good match among members, the organization, the workplace, and the policies and norms that control how the workplace is used and altered as times change. We have a long way to go to make this a reality, but I think it is worth it. My own enthusiasm may have this viewpoint playing a larger part than many managers feel is possible or necessary. If so, I think they miss the point of the cumulative impact of the work setting and its strengths for affecting other aspects of work life in organizations.

About the Author

FRITZ STEELE is a Boston-based organizational consultant and a principal in the Portsmouth Consulting Group (PCG) of Durham, New Hampshire. He has consulted for more than twenty years to a wide variety of clients on projects concerning organizational effectiveness and organizational ecology. He received his Ph.D. in Organization Studies from the Sloan School of Management at the Massachusetts Institute of Technology. He has taught organizational behavior at Yale University and at the Graduate School of Education at Harvard University. He is also an instructor in the summer programs at the Harvard Graduate School of Design.

Dr. Steele has written a number of books related to professional consulting practice and organizational change including *Physical Settings and Organization Development*, (Addison-Wesley, 1973), *The Feel of the Workplace*, with Steve Jenks (Addison-Wesley, 1977), and *The Sense of Place* (Van Nostrand Reinhold, 1981).

Index

Index

Accessibility
   of executives to organization,
      166–68
   impact on energy levels, 106–7
   productivity and, 113
Allen, Thomas, 93–94
Allocation of resources
   generalizations concerning, 191
   human systems dynamics and,
      128, 130
Ambient environment features
   amount of pleasure in setting and,
      148–49
   energy levels and, 104–5
   lighting, 127, 129–34, 180, 181
   noise, 50, 92, 97–98
   office of the future, 180–81
   temperature controls, 50, 104–5,
      181
Assumptions, organizational, xii–xiii,
      40–43
   congruence with other organiza-
      tional values, 42–43
   encouragement of feedback, 42
   minimum constraints with maxi-
      mum choice, 41
   overall goals and, 41
   quality of decision-making pro-
      cesses, 41
   support of users' experimentation,
      42
   training and development function,
      177

Bevans, Bill, 179–81
Boundary relations, 5, 137–45
   in assignment of departmental ter-
      ritories, 26
   design problems regarding, 9
   generalizations concerning, 192
   between headquarters and field
      groups, 141–44
   human systems dynamics and, 128,
      129
   intragroup effects, 138–41
   between organization and its en-
      vironment, 144
   power and, 125
Budgeting, 44
Building-wide facilities, 46

Casual contacts
   described, 90
   influences of setting on, 92–94
Cave and court design
   described, 98
   for executives, 166
   generalizations concerning, 191
Central Beheer, 86–87
Closed-plan layouts
   open-plan layouts versus, 9, 25–26,
      28
   privacy in, 97–98
Color, energy levels and, 105–6
Committees, construction and, 69, 70
Communications
   committees for problems of, 69, 70

Oshry, Barry, 100
Ownership
  executive area layout and, 160
  identity and sense of, 86–88
  participative decision making and,
    57

Participative approach
  advantages and disadvantages of,
    60
  changing user expectations and,
    186–87
  to decision making, 55, 56, 57
  in new facilities development,
    68–70
  in ongoing management of facili-
    ties, 42–43
  quality of work life and, 151–52
  role of non-managerial members
    in, 59–60
  role of specialists in, 61
Partitions, 5
Periodic programming process, 43–44
Personal preferences, 66, 67
Pile, John, 117
Planning
  managers' roles in, 56, 58–59
  for office moves, 72–74
  in ongoing facilities management,
    44
  participative approach to, 59–60
  professionals' role in, 60–62
  top executives' role in, 48–58
Plants, 7
Pleasure, organizational climate and,
    147, 148–49
Policies, 30–32
  defined, 30
  problems of, 32
  types of, 30–32
  for use of facilities, 17
  value of, 35
Positional behavior, 128, 130
Power, 119–36
  acquisition of, through settings,
    123–24
  defined, 119

human systems dynamics and,
    128–35
  impact on energy levels, 103
  in participative versus nonpartici-
    pative management, 42–43
  in settings and events, 126–28
  settings as elements of, 124–26
  settings as symbols of, 120–23
  size of workplace and, 115–16
  top-down decision-making and,
    12–13, 44, 55
Privacy
  executive area layout and, 161
  social interaction versus, 92, 97–98
Productivity, 109–18
  analyzing design relationships and,
    109–11
  defining tasks and, 111–12
  design dimensions affecting, 112–18
  problems of measuring, 110
  of training and development func-
    tion, 177
Professional facilities specialists, 60–62
  data collection by, 66
  external, 62
  internal, 61
Programming data, 66
Puttering, power and, 124

Quality of work life (QWL), 150–52.
  See also Organizational climate

Relationship management, 71
Relative location. See Location, in-
    tracompany
Resource allocation. See Allocation
  of resources
Rules
  of organizational subunits, 32–33
  for use of facilities, 17
  value of, 35

Seating arrangement
  as power and status symbol, 122
  social interaction and, 94
Security, as power and status symbol,
    122